UP-LOT REVERIES:

An Oral History of the North Fork

UP-LOT REVERIES:

An Oral History of the North Fork

By
Maria Parson

With Photographs by
Judy Ahrens

Amereon House
MATTITUCK

Most of these articles and photographs appeared previously in The Suffolk Times of Greenport, New York and The News-Review of Riverhead, New York.

Grateful acknowledgement is made to Troy and Joan Gustavson, Publishers of these fine newspapers.

A Network Project

International Standard Book Number 0-8488-0122-9

To order contact
AMEREON HOUSE, the publishing division of
Amereon Ltd.
Postal Box 1200
Mattituck, New York 11952

*Manufactured in the United States of America
by The Mad Printers of Mattituck*

To my grandparents,
Elvera and Jesse,
Annie and Tate.

Table of Contents

Introduction

This book is offered as a legacy for all who love the North Fork and all who will love it in years to come.

I did not write it, though my name is on the cover as its author. More accurate to say I wrote it down. For it is the people within its pages who truly wrote this narrative, and in lending me the privilege of recording their stories, gave us all a very special gift.

The inspiration for this book, which was first published as an on-going series in the *Suffolk Times* and *News Review*, came from my own childhood. Like most of the people you will meet here, I too grew up on Long Island. But it was an area quite different from the North Fork.

Paved over and densely populated, the suburban neighborhood I was raised in bore scant resemblance to the countryside from which it had been carved. Still, each spring, wild potatoes could be counted on to volunteer their way into our carefully manicured backyards. Undersized and misshapen, these feral reminders of the area's long-vanished farms never failed to impart a feeling of rural nostalgia in this young girl's heart. What, I wondered, had it been like before the tract houses took over? Who had lived there? And why did I feel such a loss for having missed it all?

When I was grown, I left suburbia, and later, in a quest to establish rural roots of our own, my husband and I moved to the Eastern End of Long Island, settling first in Amagansett in 1972 and later in Greenport. In 1979 we purchased an old historic home in Northville. It was in this tiny Riverhead farming community that my interest in recording the lives of those who have lived here longest began. For what better place to begin was there than in a community whose families could proudly trace their lineage back to land allotments granted to them in 1661?

In planning for this project I remembered back to the day when a friend found me with my nose buried in a book and asked what I was reading. "History," I told her. "History!" she sniffed. "Do you know what history is? It's nothing but his-story and her-story, and its telling always depends on whose side they were on!"

True enough. And so I began this book knowing that I wasn't interested in the facts and figures usually found in history books. It was not to be a rehash of the glorious battles of the Revolution fought off our shores or a compendium of significant dates and newsworthy events. Rather, I was looking for an accounting, in their own words, of all the mundane and important incidents that make up and shape everyday people's lives. If you can call the people in this book "everyday." For all have lived rich, full lives.

The youngest person you will meet here is 67, the oldest was 100 when I interviewed her. And though when contacted each protested that they really had little to say, all came through with delightfully detailed memories dating back to the North Fork at the turn-of-the-century and beyond. Many of my subjects were area natives, some were newcomers who'd only been here for 50 years or more. Then, because I was unsure of the direction these interviews were going, I decided not to start with my neighbors in Northville, but rather with a wonderful 86-year-old resident of the San Simeon by the Sound Adult Home, Mae Klipp of Greenport.

I don't know who was more nervous, Miss Klipp or I. She, after all, was not in the habit of being interviewed. And I had never conducted an interview quite like it before. But we settled in quickly as Mae, with a mischievous twinkle in her eye, described growing up in one of the town's long-gone landmarks, the Klipp House on Main Street.

It wasn't hard to find additional people to interview for this project. Some I'd known for years. Others were suggested to me by their friends and relatives. Doubtless there are hundreds of other stories out there waiting to be told, and I am sure that every reader will be able to think of several people who might have been included. For in my opinion, it is the people of the North Fork who are its greatest natural resource. But it is a finite one. And in many cases as the old ones pass away, so too do their stories. Stories and memories considered not important, perhaps, in the context of history, yet integral in the shaping of the character and fiber of the North Fork. Perhaps that is why I felt such a sense of urgency in finishing this book.

Many people deserve credit for its creation. First and foremost, the people in it, for graciously allowing me to get to know them, if only for a little while. And Troy and Joan Gustavson, co-publishers for the *Suffolk Times* and *News Review*, who agreed that the concept was a good one and saw fit to allow it space in their newspapers. Then there is Judy Ahrens, a brilliant photographer and trusted friend. Only an artist so focused on her work could have captured the essence of the people you will meet here as she did. Last, I want to thank the many readers who took an interest in this series, encouraging me with their letters and calls. None of this could have happened without all of you.

Maria Parson
Northville, L. I., N. Y.

In Case You're Wondering . . .

when a man was going out to farm he might say "I'm going up-lot now," or "I'm going down-lot," and you knew he was either headed north or south. I grew up thinking everybody in the world thought that north was up-lot and south was down-lot . . . the word came from the word allotment — . . . the early settlers had each been granted certain allotments of land at a town meeting in 1661. They had just shortened the word to lot, then added up-lot or down-lot to indicate direction.

— Estelle Evans

and now . . .
on with the Reveries

Mae Klipp

Mae Klipp

Mae Klipp was born in Greenport on May 29, 1898. When she was three years old, her family moved to the mansard roofed mansion which was to be her home for the next 72 years. Miss Klipp, who never married, lived in the 18-room house until 1975. A year later, the 150-year-old residence on Greenport's Main Street was demolished to make way for a bank. Currently a resident of the San Simeon by the Sound Adult Home in Greenport, Miss Klipp offered these reminiscences of a lifetime spent on the North Fork.

I was a seven month baby — what they call premature. When I was born they put me in a cigar box and put it behind the stove to keep me warm. 'Course, I don't remember it, but my sisters were always tellin' me about how I kept my arms and legs all tucked up to my chest for the first two months and then I straightened out, just like that. My mother never thought I would live, but I did.

There were seven of us, six girls and a boy. Now there's only two of us left. Me and my sister Lena. She's here too and she'll be 100 in June. Me and Lena, we're fightin' to outlive each other.

I was born in Greenport and have lived here all my life. We had a home, it was the one between the two banks, but I was born in the house across from the Methodist Church. We moved to our new house —the one folks call the Klipp house, in 1901.

THE KLIPP HOUSE NEXT DOOR TO THE PEOPLE'S BANK, LATER THE NORTH FORK BANK & TRUST CO.

My father, Fred Klipp, worked on the water. He had a boat and he used to cart fish until one day he fell overboard. He didn't drown, but that helped him decide to go into another line of work, so he went into the tobacco business. My father made cigars in Greenport. You know where the photographer's shop is on Main Street? Next door was his place. And the Arcade, that used to be his place too. I used to help him out in the shop, pulling stems off the leaves of tobacco

18   **Up-Lot Reveries**

and then rolling them up. I used to smoke cigarettes but I stopped last July. My sister, she was always tellin' me, "Please stop smokin'. Please stop smokin'," and I'd always tell her, "I won't stop smokin' till the day I die. They can put a pack in my coffin." But then, a friend of mine passed on and before she died she was always tellin' me to stop smokin' so after I went to her funeral I said maybe I'll try it. I used to smoke Benson & Hedges but I started out on Chesterfields. I used to smoke three packs a day 'cause I was in the business.

FRED KLIPP

I could've married, but I didn't. Too independent, I guess. I worked all of my life. The first job I ever had, I sold tickets in the movie house. That's where Auricchio's is now. They showed silent movies back in those days. I didn't have any favorite movie stars. Years back you didn't care. If there was nothin' doin' you went to the movies. I used to go to dances, stay out till three, come home and go to work. My father used to say to my mother, "Is Polly home yet?" — he used to call me Polly — and she'd say no. And when I'd come home he'd call out and ask me what time it was and I'd tell him, "Oh, it's 10 o'clock," even when it was close to dawn. I used to love to go to dances and I never waited for a man to take me. If I got one, fine. I think the dances today are okay but they don't dance like we used to. Now they do what I'd call the hoppy hop.

In the olden days we had horses and wagons and when it stormed the water would come up into the town from the bay. We were a family that kept very close. My father never hit us or anything but he brought us up to know what's right and what's wrong. Our house was a good place to grow up in. There was lots of rooms and plenty of steps and bannisters to slide down. I fell down the stairs three times doin' that. When I was a little girl I always wore dresses. I never wore pants until I came up here. I still wear dresses once in awhile now 'cause I don't want to get too used to pants.

One year right around Christmastime my sister's husband was killed in an accident. Now at that time of the year we'd have the house all decorated with each of the rooms done up in a different color. When the news of the accident reached us we took all the decorations down in two hours flat. My mother was one of those kinds that if there was any trouble or sickness she made sure we all behaved until the problem was over. She was the one who taught me not to be afraid of dead people. I used to be scared stiff and wouldn't look at them. When my grandfather died she took me in to see him and showed me there was nothin' to be afraid of. All of our people were buried from home. We'd lay them out in the parlor. It's kind

Up-Lot Reveries

of strange thinkin' that in the end I had to come up here to live — not that everybody isn't real nice to me here. I felt real bad when I had to sell the house, but it was 18 rooms and I just couldn't keep up with it.

I watch TV every night. I love ball games. I used to watch the Mets and the Yankees. When the Mets went downhill I watched the Yankees. Then they weren't any better than the Mets. The Series was good this year. Maybe next year if I'm alive I'll see the Mets pick up.

How come some of us old timers have lived so long? I don't know. I try to stay healthy but one thing I don't believe in is exercise. I don't think it's good for your heart. And I never eat fish. Give me rare beef every day of the week. I was born with a veil over my face — that's supposed to be lucky. I think I've been lucky. I've lived to be 84 years old. I think that's lucky, don't you?

— February 24, 1983

Ella Wells

Ella Wells

The Wells farm in Riverhead has been owned by the Wells family since 1661 and has been designated the oldest family-run farm in New York State. Mrs. Ella Wells, widow of Vernon Wells Sr., is the family matriarch. Mrs. Wells offered these memories of her early years on the farm.

I was born at home on Sound Avenue in the house I grew up in. You weren't born anywhere else way back then. My mother lost her first two babies and then when my brother was born she just couldn't believe he would live, but he did. Then she had my sister and then me. My father was a farmer. He was born right down the road here on the old Wells strip.

My parent's weren't strict but they did make me toe the mark. They had what they called a "little doctor" — it was really a little riding whip — hanging up by the kitchen door. I can remember having my father look at me in church when I was being a little unruly and having him remind me about the little doctor hanging up at home. Then I'd sit up and pay attention, at least for awhile. We were brought up going to church on Sundays and I loved it because I could put on my good clothes. You see, we didn't keep good clothes on all day. Now you dress the same way in the morning as you do in the afternoon, unless you want to go to a real party at night which I don't go to at this age. We'd even change our petticoats after church. We'd take off our good things and put on our ordinary clothes. Same went for school. We kept our school dresses good. We used to wear pinafore aprons over them to keep them nice.

DISTRICT #10 SCHOOLHOUSE, NORTHVILLE, ELLA WELLS IS THIRD FROM THE LEFT

Sound Avenue was a dirt road back in those days and it used to be kinda fun when spring came and the horses would almost get stuck pulling their feet in and

Up-Lot Reveries

out of the mud.

I went to grade school at the Northville School, where Long Island Kitchens is now, and I remember one time we were driving along to school and the man who was taking us was making the horse go pretty good because we were already late as it was. So he was giving the horse some extra encouragement and the horse dropped dead in the road. Oh, it was the worst thing, but that day we walked the rest of the way as slow as we wanted to because we knew we had a good excuse.

Childhood was a lot of fun back in those days. When it snowed we had a sled they called a pung, and the horse would pull it right along the ground. My brother, Leslie, once made a sidecar for his bicycle and he would take me along in it. He was always making things. Leslie used to love to experiment with electricity at the local Y. We'd all go over there with him and stand around in a circle and let him give us a shock.

We used to keep beef cattle in the barn and then a butcher from Riverhead would come and kill them. My father used to go around from Port Jefferson to Greenport picking up calves. I loved those calves. I once had one small enough to push in a doll carriage. I didn't ever see its finish because I was too attached to him. But you have to be sensible when you live on a farm, like my kids are.

My son, Vernon Jr., had a calf and he took care of it and it grew up and when it had its first calf, the cow died. We dragged it off to the clay pit and I remember little Vernon saying to me that night, "Mom, it would surprise us if we saw that cow coming around the barn, wouldn't it?" And it would have. You try to explain things as best you can to children and I recall I was once trying to tell Vernon about how nothing lives forever and he turned to me and he said, "But momma, if we're all going to die, why be born?" I've thought of that a million times since that day when he was four right up to now.

We didn't have running water in our home when I was growing up. We took baths in the kitchen in a wooden tub and we didn't change our clothes everyday. Somehow we lived through.

We had a cistern at school, same as at home, and in the wintertime we'd bring a pail of water into the classroom and everybody would drink from it. We all lived through that too — at least most of us did.

The Wells tract was granted in 1661. My family never spoke much about our history. We just worked. But people have been coming around here to interview us ever since 1966. I said to someone the other day I don't know what I can tell anyone I haven't already told someone else before, yet there's always something. I have to reach way back in my memory for some things, but none of it seems like it happened all that long ago. I'll be 82 next month. It's a very funny thing, this getting old. Things happen — good and bad — and you just have to take them in your stride and go on living.

— March 10, 1983

Ralph Tuthill

Ralph Tuthill

Ralph Tuthill served as Southold Town Justice for 21 years. He recalls marrying at least 100 couples, as well as performing many less romantic duties in his job as justice of the Peace.

I was born on Elijah's Lane in Mattituck on April 20, 1896. I had five brothers and a sister, so I didn't lack for company too much. In 1900, when I was four years old, my brother Jay was born. I remember I came down through my mother's bedroom and she says, "Look here," and she pulls down the covers and there was Jay. So I says, "Where'd he come from," and she tells me, "Oh, Dr. Pete brought him in his satchel..." And I believed her.

My father was a farmer, so of course we kids had certain chores to do, but I didn't object to it. My pop was the perfect slave driver. I was already milking a cow when I was eight years old, and we had calves to feed and chickens to get the eggs from when we got home from school. My pop used to give me two cents each for raising baby chickens and I'd make a dollar or two that way. We had a dairy beginning in 1909 or '10.

My mother's name was Carrie Case Tuthill and she had seven children. It was really a shame — She was just 52 years old and had just gotten to where the kids were big enough so she could go out and drive a horse by herself and she got cancer. They did a mastectomy on her at a big hospital in Rockville Centre in 1914, but after a few years she died.

When my mother died — that was in January of 1916 — my sister Edith took over. She was a good cook and then she went and got married in December of 1916. When she left, my brother Jay and I were alone with my father. My father used to go down to New Suffolk to a livery stable owned by two of my brothers and he'd stay there nights. So the day my sister left, Jay and I was wondering what the devil we were going to eat. Well, the next morning we had corn flakes and milk and things like that, and my dad, well he'd come home in the daytime and fry up potatoes. We got along very good.

My brother Frank, he'd gone to Southold Academy in 1900 and learned stenography and typewriting because at that time girls weren't in the office like they are now. He worked in Grand Central Station in New York. It was one of his friends that convinced me I should join the U. S. Navy and on August 2, 1917, I enlisted. I was stationed at the 52nd Street Armory in Brooklyn and from there 21 of us were chosen to go on board the **Martha Washington**, a captured Austrian passenger ship that was being converted for use as a troop carrier. Eventually, we went to France and crossed the ocean 18 times bringing troops over there. We used to carry depth bombs and if the ship wasn't going at least 14 knots an hour you'd blow yourself up. I'll always remember the first time I went ashore and heard the French people with their wooden shoes. My friend Harold Grathwohl was with me. He and I always stuck together. We even went into the Navy together.

I got married in 1920. My wife's name was Laura Fanning and I knew her from the time she was a girl and we used to go to Sunday school together. We went courting in a horse-drawn wagon. Sometimes I'd take her to Library Hall. That was just west of where the "Coffee Pot" is now. There was a basketball court and theater that could hold 700 people. One time I took out Lois Fischer — she's the mother of Otis Pike, our former congressman. I took her to a dance in Southold. Of course, in 1916 I got a car and me and Harold Grathwohl would take the girls out in it. Laura and I had four children, two girls and two boys. One of my grandsons is in the Peace Corps in Zaire working in a fish hatchery.

When Judge Case of Cutchogue died in 1947, George Tuthill came along and asked if I'd take the job. So I told him, "I don't know anything about being a justice of the peace," and he said, "Oh, you can handle it," so I said, "Okay."

I worked into it gradually but I was really scared at first. Eventually I was handling around 600 cases a year and got over my nerves pretty much. One case I'll never forget — a woman came to me and said she wanted her husband arrested. So I says, "Does he drink?" and she says, "No," "Does he beat you up?" No, again. So I asked her, "Well, what's the trouble?"

and she says, "Well, he wants too much sex!" I says, "Forget it." I'm staying out of that one."

Otto Anrig was chief of police then and we only had two or three policemen. I held court on Elijah's Lane at our farm. Then in '48 I bought the Nat Tuthill farm. We moved into a 20-room house and I had a nice little office in the northeast corner. All the Town paid for was the telephone. I must'a married 100 couples. One couple I remember come in on a Sunday afternoon and it was snowing like the devil outside. Now in order for girls to be married they had to be 18 and she wasn't quite there yet. So I called up the minister from the Presbyterian Church in Cutchogue and he came and married them. And the fellow, he was so very glad to get married — which I guess was a good idea — that he gave me a check for $25 which I gave to the preacher and he gave to the church.

Otto Anrig called me at 5 o'clock in the morning one time and he says, "I just caught a bunch of kids shooting craps. Get down here and bring your book." I guess 20 people went before me that morning and I fined them all $5. Every once in awhile I meet one of them now and they always yell at me, "Five dollars!" . . . But I think they took it pretty good.

I'm an old potato farmer and dairy man, but I think grapes are the coming thing. The potato farmers last year had a very bad year. You can't blame farmers for selling out to developers, but I'd like to see them stay on. This year, the ones who can weather it, why they'll stay on and hope. As far as Southold Town, I hope they don't get too many houses out here. I think they should keep some open land. Just the other day I was thinking about Jim Grattan. Now, around 1906 or '07, Jim used to come through town herding cattle along

34   **Up-Lot Reveries**

the main road. It's hard to believe, isn't it? Think about what would happen to any poor cow that got out there today.

I never really thought about whether I'd ever get this old or not. I try to have a lot of interests. Being the Justice of the Peace, I met a lot of people and they still remember me. I still drive a car and ride a bicycle. I rode four miles yesterday. I try to exercise and not drink too much coffee. I stopped smoking in 1933. I'm an optimist not a pessimist and I'm not discouraged. Some people think the world is going to the devil, but I don't think that way.

— *April 14, 1983*

Harry Edwards

Snapshot from an old family album

Harry Edwards

Retired farmer Harry Edwards of Calverton was interviewed in a home about half a mile from his birthplace. Though confined to a wheelchair, Mr. Edwards offered several lively reminscences including an eye-witness account of the Old Golden Pickle Works train wreck in 1926.

I was born on March 17, 1900, on Edwards Avenue in Calverton. The house is gone now, but my grandfather lived in there. Edwards Avenue was a dirt road then and it got so muddy in the spring that no one could go on it. Then we got a new Town Supervisor and his platform was to concrete the road to Jamesport and Edwards Avenue, and so they did. It was quite an improvement. I remember a time before that when Johnny Reitmeir got his wagon stuck in the mud. His horse went down, too. Johnny used to deliver margarine around here.

My mother's name was Grace Carter. She went to work when they had the cranberry marsh down here. Brown's Marsh, they called it. She went there and that was the only place she ever worked outside of her home. She never went anywhere else. There used to be a lot of flies around here because of the cows and pigs and horses. I remember my mother had a big swatter kind of thing and I'd hold the door while she chased the flies out.

My father, Fred, was a carpenter. He and George Reeve built the house next door to here in 1903. I had a brother. When I was a young boy, of course we didn't have any television, so for fun we played cards and ate peanuts. My parents were great card sharks, too.

I had an 87-acre farm on Fresh Pond Avenue that I cleared myself and then the government condemned it for Grumman. We used horses for plowing before we got tractors. I bought my first car, a Model T, from the same dealer we bought the tractors from. I wish I had it now. We used to buy horses from Frank Corwin. William Post from East Williston used to ship them out to Frank in Riverhead and he would auction them off. They usually had distemper by the time they got here. We got medicine from the vet and cured them up.

I was a farmer all my life, all my life until I had my legs taken off. That was 15 or 20 years ago. I haven't slept a wink since. I don't know why, I just can't sleep. We used a lot of chemicals when I was farming and I don't think they gave us adequate warning about them, but I never suffered any bad effects from them as far as I know.

I was there when the train ran off the tracks and into the Old Golden Pickle Works. I remember I was

Up-Lot Reveries

up at the crossing of Edwards Avenue and the Main Road on my way home from work. I was looking to see if I had the time to get across the tracks before the train, when all of a sudden I saw it coming. It looked like an enormous caterpillar and then the dirt and dust flew and you couldn't see anything. I turned right around and went back there and a fella from Mattituck, he was carrying this little boy out of the wreck and he says, "Take him to the doctor in Riverhead!" The boy was only 12 years old and he died in my car on the way. Of course the pickle factory was demolished because two engines and about eight cars went right into it. Six people were killed. It was the worst thing I ever saw. Two people I knew were on the train — Nat Talmage of Baiting Hollow and his father. They came walking down off the back end looking for some other means of transportation.

Right around the time of World War I, they had a big army camp, Camp Upton, where the Brookhaven Lab is now. I remember train after trainload of soldiers going down to the Manorville station and then transferring over to Eastport and then to New York. From there they shipped out to France. I was too young to be a soldier but I did receive some military training up in the Benjamin Building in Riverhead. That's the big building on the northwest corner of Roanoke and Main Street.

My wife's name was Charlotte Stewart. I met her on a blind date in Sag Harbor and it was love at first sight. We were married on December 1, 1928, in the little church around the corner from here.

I never took a drink in my life. During Prohibition I helped the prohibition officers go after the rum-runners. We caught a boat in Greenport and we used to go to Montauk, but Montauk was a bad place, you could get killed if you went down there alone. I believed in prohibition. I think there should be laws that people can't drink because it kills people. If they can't get it, they can't drink it.

Maybe I'll live to be 100. I feel all right and I can eat three square meals a day. I can't sleep so I watch television, especially if there's any ballgames on.

The future? I don't know. They talk about the arms race and so forth, but I don't know what they'll do — whether they'll have another war or not — but I doubt it.

— April 14, 1983

Donald Gildersleeve

Donald Gildersleeve

*Donald Gildersleeve was born and raised in Mattituck,
where his family owned and operated a large grocery/
department store. He was interviewed in his Mattituck
home.*

I was born in Mattituck on December 17, 1892.
Mattituck was a small town then. My father,
James Andrew Gildersleeve, had a job in Port
Jefferson and that's where he met my mother,
Frances Hawkins. They had three or four children
while they were living there and three died in infancy.
Later they moved to Mattituck. Altogether, my mother
had 12 children and I was the baby. The only thing I
remember of my father — he died when I was three
—was one day when I was just a child, and I toddled
into his store, where I wasn't supposed to be. A man
with a black moustache swooped me up and smiled at

me — that was my father, and it's the only memory I have of him.

I started school in Mattituck when I was four years old and went from the first grade through my first year of high school but by then I was already getting very deaf. My mother, she was deaf, too. She had a long . . . what you'd call a speaking tube, and that helped a lot. Me, I went through every type of hearing aid ever made. The first one was what you call the carbon type. It had a big receiver that hung from your chest. I tried all the rest after that, but I guess for a about six years now I haven't heard a thing.

My grandfather, Andrew Gildersleeve, was from Middle Island. He lived on a farm and by the time he was 12 years old he was already doing farm work. Then he learned the shoemaker's trade and later apprenticed out for several years as a carpenter. After he'd finished his apprenticeship, he bought a good suit of clothes and a chest of tools and started a business as a journeyman carpenter. The highest he ever got paid at that time was 71 cents a day. Eventually he got out to Cutchogue and Mattituck and raised his family there.

My grandfather built several buildings in Mattituck including the Presbyterian Church. In 1854 he built the Octagon Building on the corner of Love Lane. At that time there was a store on Pike Street owned by Barnabus Pike. It was a big store, a long two-story. My grandfather bought it and went into business with Mr. John Wills. Then my grandfather died and my father and his brother, Arthur, took over the store together. You know where all those shops are now on Pike Street? I mean the hairdresser and those other shops? Well, that's where the Gildersleeve Store was.

It took up a whole block. We sold everything from groceries to overalls to workclothes to ladies' wear —even corsets. There was also shoes, notions, hardware — and that was just on the first floor.

When I was a boy there was no fire department. There was bucket brigades. One night the store across the railroad tracks from our store burned down. 'Course there was no organization. Between our store and our house there was an old fashioned water pump with a wooden handle and the night of the fire they pumped it dry. After that, there began to be a demand for a fire department and one was organized in 1905, I think. They bought an old second-hand pumper, the handle was about so long, and you had to pump from each side. I remember pumping it once or twice.

When I was 19, I joined the department and the first night I joined the annual meeting for election of officers and so forth was going on. A chum of mine, a fellow by the name of Wickham, had been the secretary-treasurer for the company and when he came up for nomination he said, "Oh, I nominate Donald Gildersleeve." He was sick of the job and he was my chum so he picked on me! I held that job for 33 years. And then in 1932 or so the whole thing was reorganized and they had to have a board of commissioners and a secretary-treasurer, so they offered it to me. I had that second job for 32 years.

I remember several big fires — one of them in our own barn. Our store did deliveries, you know — took orders and delivered them. We had four horses, with six stables and a storage shed. Upstairs was a hayloft and next to that was a cow shed with one cow. Next to the cow shed was a hog pen and we kept two hogs in there. We lost them all in that fire. After the barn burned down there was a big bare strip and my brother says how'd you like to grow some vegetables in there? So I did, but they didn't turn out, except the carrots. After that I saw an advertisement for tulip bulbs so I bought some and they came up just like that. Then I saw an ad for rose bushes. I'd never raised them before but they thrived. Before long I had near 100 bushes. I had a wonderful time. Our house was next door to our store so I'd go out and cut a few roses and put them in a vase on the counter and then give them to customers to take along. I made a lot of friends through those roses. When I married I moved and I dug up most of them by hand and took them with me.

The Mattituck Literary Society was organized in my father's time. It was on Pike Street, just east of where the "Coffee Pot" is now. Every Tuesday night they'd have a program followed by dancing. The programs might be music or short plays and skits. It cost 25 cents for members and 50 cents for non-members. You ought to have seen some of those summer people crabbin' because they had to pay 50 cents. One thing if you didn't have a program, then no dancing.

I remember one day a woman, she had tried hard to get a program together and wasn't having any luck. Some people liked to take part and some didn't. Anyway, she came around with a little skit and asked me if I'd take part in it. It was just a three-page script, and that night me and two of my friends got up there and performed it. We got through the first page just fine. Then we lost track of where we were. I was deaf and there was a girl standing in the wings trying to prompt me. She kept giving me a cue, but the only line I could think of was "I must catch that train." Finally the curtain came down and and she stormed up to me and said, "I hate you!" Well, that wasn't in the script at all. When it was over, me and my friends grabbed each other and laughed and laughed. Literary Hall kept going until around World War I, but then there weren't enough fellas around for the dancin' and some years later it was torn down.

Even though my hearing's gone, my eyes are still good, though my right eye's getting weaker. They used to have a song around here that went:
"Left little eye is a good little eye, But my right eye likes to roam. If they don't stop making them so beautiful, I'll have to leave my right eye home."

Did I ever think I'd live to be 90? I never gave it a thought. You come and you go.

The North Fork? I think vineyards are the coming thing. Potatoes seem to be going out. 'Course Alice and I, we're temperance people, but the farmers got to make a living, don't you think?

— *April 28, 1983*

An Oral History of the North Fork   49

John and Edith Courtenay

John and Edith Courtenay

*Riverhead native John Courtenay and his wife Edith live
in Greenport in an historic home which was passed down
from Mrs. Courtenay's late husband, Herbert Corwin.*

John Courtenay: I'm of English descent.
They had seven generations of John Court-
enays over there. No juniors, you know, and
there were seven of them. I was the eighth,
and my son is the ninth, and his son is the
tenth, and his son is the eleventh. We got eleven of 'em
now.

I was born on Hamilton Avenue in Riverhead on
Sept. 16, 1893. I had two brothers and four sisters. My
mother surprised us all by having my last little sister
20 years after she was through having the rest of us.
She was 46 at the time. What was is it like growing up
in Riverhead? Wonderful! We lived one block away

from what used to be the Suffolk County Fairgrounds and they had a half mile track for harness racing in the summertime. 'Course we didn't have a horse. We walked. My father had a bicycle to go to work on. If he was workin' out of town he'd hire a horse and wagon from the livery.

We went swimmin' in the summertime. We didn't go swimmin' in the wintertime 'cept when we fell in. My brother did, once. Up near Middle Road there was a big pond in the woods and this one Sunday my father said, "Well boys, now what're you gonna do?" So we said, "Oh, we're just gonna take a walk." He says, "Don't get in any trouble and don't go on the ice." So we got up to this pond and, as we approached, the trees were all on the south side shading it and of course it was all frozen there. I guess there was six or eight of us boys. So my younger brother says, "I'll be the first to cross the pond!" and he started runnin' and got to going so fast that he couldn't stop and he skidded right into the water. Luckily, it wasn't too deep and he walked to shore on the other side.

So instead of going home he went to our friend's house and my friend's mother had him take off his clothes and she put 'em round the back of the stove to dry off. He came home afterwards all dry and none of us ever said anything about it, but I think he finally did tell our mother and father about it several years later.

I lived in Riverhead until I was 27 and then I got married and moved to Peconic. I was married to my first wife for 49 years, and I've been married to Edith for the past 22. It'll be 23 in November. You say I've been married most of my life? Not most of it. I didn't get married until I was 27 years old. I had some life before that, you know. Nowadays people don't want to get married and they don't. I don't think it's natural.

I was in the Navy in World War I, enlisted in New York City and got shipped to Pensacola, Florida. I was signed up to go overseas but about three days before we were supposed to leave I got the flu and I was in the base hospital for seven weeks. So I missed going over, but it's just as well. I wouldn't have won the war over there for 'em.

Edith Courtenay: "You know, that's singular in a way, because my first husband, Herbert Corwin, was saved from going overseas because he was sent down to the Mexican border in 1914 and down there he contracted typhoid fever and it left him in such a debilitated state that he didn't get sent over either.

John Courtenay: In those days we used to go shopping once a week. We didn't have to go everyday like they do now. My wife would make up a list and I'd stop and pick up the groceries on my way home from work. A week's worth of groceries would run us around $19. I was a carpenter and from 1922 until 1933 there wasn't any question a'tall about making a living. I had a job all the time. But from 1933 to 1940 I couldn't find one. That was during the depression. We took all our money out of the bank. We didn't have any trouble getting food, of course. If a neighbor had some beans, why they'd come over and say, "we got string beans, come over and pick yourself a mess." We couldn't buy a lot, but we didn't need it. We wasn't educated that way.

In a few months I'll be 90. I never figured on living to be 100, and I know I won't. The way I feel the last couple of days I don't think I'll even make the week.

Edith Courtenay: That's why he's out there raking leaves . . . The first time he came here, he stopped by to

An Oral History of the North Fork   55

sharpen a saw for me. We were married in 1961 and John has done so much to make this old house comfortable. I always like to kid him by telling him that he married me just because I'm a good cook, and he always says, "I'm not denying that it helped." Here's a strange thing. Both of my husbands were born one day apart in the same year. I met my first husband, Mr. Corwin, when he was a patient in the hospital in which I was doing my nurse's training —Swedish Hospital in New York. He had just come back from the Mexican border with typhoid fever and I didn't have anything to do with him when he was a patient. However when he got well and came back to visit he picked me out and hounded me. We were engaged in April, 1917, and in June he said, "I want you to come down to Greenport."

I told him I would have to write to my mother in New Haven and ask her if it would be all right for me to do that. I was 22 at the time. I also told him that he would have to get his mother to write a letter asking me to come, and he did. I was met at the Greenport train station by a surrey with fringe on top driven by a Mr. Black, who was the taxi driver of the day, and transported up here in style.

I had the most wonderful week. For recreation Mr. Corwin took me rowing. One night we came in about nine o'clock and his mother was horrified. She said, "What are you doing keeping a girl out there in the dark? What will people say? Don't you know you must guard her reputation?" My mother-in-law was very strict. My husband's father was Captain Addison Corwin and he was very well respected in the town.

This house was built in 1843. This street was called Tuthill Street then, after the man who built this house

Up-Lot Reveries

and they should have kept it that way. Herbert and I used to come down here weekends and summers. Our lad, Jim, spent every summer of his life from the time he was four years old down here. I remember him standing out on the breakwater one day and he said, "Mommy, I love all of this — the water, the rocks, the sea — everything!" I moved here permanently in 1958.

Sometimes I think back to when I was a girl. I washed clothes on the washboard and we wore stiffly starched collars which I would iron like a professional. Today with all the no-iron there's nothing to do. Once in awhile I do iron a damask tablecloth because we are people who like a nicely set table with dinner napkins and sterling silver rings. People say, oh no, don't give me a linen napkin, a paper one will do. I tell them, "When you're in my house you take what you get."

— *May 12, 1983*

Eva Woodward

Eva Woodward

Mattituck's Eva Woodward, 96, is well known locally for the vegetables and berries grown in her large summer garden. The mother of seven, Mrs. Woodward had 38 grandchildren and 48 great-grandchildren at last count.

I was born in Northport on January 12, 1887. I was 96 last January. My father was the owner and publisher of *The Northport Journal*. After I left school, I worked in my father's office running the presses and setting type. We had to set each letter by hand, line for line. I met my husband there. He was a printer.

My husband and I were married in 1906 and we moved to Mattituck in 1919. This is the only house I've ever lived in in Mattituck and it was already 100 years old when we got here. My husband worked at the *Riverhead Review*. When we moved here we didn't even have a hand pump in the kitchen. No improvements. In those days you washed and ironed by hand. We heated our irons on the stove and we lived here six years before we got electricity. We pumped water outside, brought it in and washed clothes on a board in the tub. If you don't think that's hard work, you should try it.

We had seven children, all born at home. Everybody had babies at home in those days. They weren't forced to go to the hospital like they are now. When my first one was born, I had an aunt, and she was a midwife and could deliver a baby as good as any doctor. 'Course, if there was an emergency, your doctor would come to the house. Now, they won't come, no matter what's the matter.

There was so much to do when I was raising my family that in the evening I didn't get to bed until way after midnight. The ironing was tremendous. And my boys, they had a name here in Mattituck. They all wore white shirts to school everyday. So the ironing was very heavy and besides that I baked five loaves of bread every other day.

I don't believe in women working outside the home unless they have to. 'Course, sometimes they have to, but I think that parents today have changed more than children. They're not parents anymore — some of them, anyway. Now, with all I had to do, I took the time after supper with my children to read them stories. With the older ones we played games — card games and monopoly.

I tell you, I could write a book about some of the things that have happened over the years. My father, for instance, disappeared in 1911. He not only had the newspaper, he had a store, and his Christmas goods hadn't come in. So he went to New York to find out

Up-Lot Reveries

why and he never reached the city, and nobody ever heard from him. My mother took it hard at the time, but she got over it. Then he came back in 1925. Don't any of us know exactly where he was all that time, and he said he couldn't remember.

I've always been well but last Christmastime I was sick and I just lost all my strength. I doctored myself 'til I was getting better and then they all made such a fuss that I should go to the doctor. So I went, but what he gave me didn't do any more good than what I was doing for myself. I went down to eighty-something pounds before I started to get better, but I'm still not very steady on my feet.

I work in my garden every day. How do I do it? Just faith that I'll be able to do as much as possible. I always was ambitious. It never agreed with me to sit around. At the beginning of the season I couldn't work too long in the garden because over the winter you get rusty, as they say. Now I come out in the morning at eight-and-a half past and stay 'til noon. I don't do much in the afternoon — just a little bit.

I haven't planted much yet this year. I put out some tomatoes but it was too cold. I usually have two or three dozen squash. I used to have a great big garden. Now I have currant bushes and sell currants to people who like to make currant jelly. And raspberries — I'm known as the raspberry lady. I could sell more, but I've slowed down so.

These are my raspberries. I cut them back, but not too much. If you do, you cut all your raspberries off. I fertilize them with dehydrated cow manure and the regular 10-5. See those wild onions? When I pull them up, instead of throwing them down where they're going to grow again next season, I put them in bags and send them off to the dump. I planted those lilacs several years ago and this is the first time they've had a blossom. Do I plant by the full moon? I plant when I'm ready to. Talking to plants? Well, I've never tried it, but I don't know. I'm afraid they wouldn't understand me. I'm very fond of all outdoor work. I painted the porch four years ago and I used to do all the painting in the house.

I like to watch the evening news on TV. As far as the world situation goes, I don't know what to say. I think we're headed for Armageddon. I think it's shaping up. May be quite awhile before it comes to a climax, but we're going to get the last war someday. I don't know why nations can't agree to stay home and mind their own business. Life is too short for the individual. It's been too short for me, in a way. You know, when you look ahead, 50 years seems to be a long time. But when you look back, it's a very short time. And the older you get, the faster time seems to go.

— May 26, 1983

Lena Gardiner

Lena Gardiner

Lena Klipp Gardiner celebrated her 100th birthday on June 4, 1983. A life-long resident of Greenport, Mrs. Gardiner grew up in the historic Klipp House, which once graced Greenport's Main Street. Currently a resident of the Sam Simeon by the Sound nursing home in Greenport, Mrs. Gardiner was aided in this interview by her daughter, Jane Sachs.

I was born in Greenport on June 4, 1883. I had five sisters and one brother. That's what I got in my family. 'Course I got a lot of different relatives around, but I don't bother monkeying with them very much. I'm the oldest and my sister Mae is the youngest. We're the only ones left now.

My father had a business in Greenport near the corner of Front and Main Streets. He made cigars. Me, I never smoked in my life. I used to help my father in the store after school. We'd go in and stem tobacco so my dad would have the leaf to make cigars. The shop had a big counter with glass over it. His workroom had a pot belly stove and he had a great big wooden Indian on the pedestal in front of the store. He sold that Indian to a fella from Shelter Island and the fella got rid of it. An actress bought it and took it across the ocean with her to Belgium.

I wasn't born in the Klipp House. We moved there when I was a young girl. My mother used to love to decorate that house. There were two double rooms in front, a parlor, and another room in back of that. My room was way up on the third floor. We had a front stoop and a side porch with wisteria vines all over it.

My mother always said I should'a been a boy instead of a girl. I was strong. I used to play baseball out in the lot with the boys. My mother never tried to stop me. She'd rather have me doin' that than being off somewhere where she couldn't find me. I went to school in Greenport where the fire department is now. The little Exempt place used to be the kindergarten. I was a good student. My mother would'a punished me if I was bad, she would'a give me a whippin'.

My baby sister Mae lives here now. She's on the go all the time. I helped take care of her when she was a baby. I used to walk her around in a carriage that had one of those, what was it? — a parasol. That's right, a parasol. It was attached to the front. She was a real cute baby — a little bit of a thing. My mother had her before it was time. She used to keep her in a box behind the woodstove so she'd stay warm. I'd go take a look at her every once in awhile. I loved her. She was a good baby.

68   **Up-Lot Reveries**

We had a nice big car. A seven passenger Lincoln with wooden spokes. We'd have the top down on it half the time. My father also had a boat and I went out on it with him. I never learned to swim — yet. I had a bathing suit with a fancy little yoke, bloomers and a skirt. I'd go out in the water with that.

I left home to work in Ruby Wiggins' boarding house in Greenport. I did the cookin' and things like that. I was married on November 18, 1910, to Parker Smith Gardiner. We're related to the Gardiners of Gardiner's Island way far back, but my husband came from Nova Scotia. He was an engineer on a pleasure yacht — the **Aztec**. When he left the boat he became a postman. He spent 27 years walking for the Greenport post office. We were married for 60 years. I had two children, a son, Frederick, and a daughter, Jane. My husband was an awful nice man. He never went to movies. We took walks together. He never danced. I loved to go to dances. He was a horrible dancer so I'd dance with other girls there. The dances were at the old post office. (Editors Note: On the corner where the parking lot of the Bank of New York is now.)

I knew Fred Corwin when he ran *The Suffolk Times*. I knew E.J. Warner. He died recently, but I knew Everett. All those people are gone now. I've outlived them all. It's the way the Lord wanted it.

Things kinda slip away from me as I grow old. You can't remember everything . . . I'm not really looking forward to my birthday party, unless maybe I can have some ice cream. I always ate plain food. My mother never cooked fancy things — just meat and potatoes. I never thought I'd live to be 100. I don't know, I just let things happen as they happen.

— *June 2, 1983*

An Oral History of the North Fork

Frances
Adams

Frances Adams

Frances Adams, 85, spent her childhood summers in Peconic at the family compound on Indian Neck Lane. Her mother, a pianist, and her father, a doctor, brought their daughter up in a world peopled with the leading artists, musicians and intellectuals of the day. "I've always been with interesting people," she says. "It just seemed to me obvious people . . . " Though she still has a house in Peconic and another in Vermont, Ms. Adams prefers to live now in a tiny Southold apartment — her "snail shell," as she puts it — comfortably surrounded by her good friends and the paintings, photographs and memorabilia of her long and fascinating life.

I was born in New York on 5th Avenue and 18th Street, but we always summered in Peconic. My grandfather had bought land on Little Peconic Bay in Indian Neck, and then he saw a house that he liked the looks of on the Main Road in Aquebogue, so he had it taken apart and moved on a barge to Peconic. To my mind, next to the Bay of Naples, Little Peconic Bay is still the most beautiful place in the world.

There were a great many artists along Indian Neck at that time, including Henry Prellwitz, Irving R. Wiles and Edwin Bell, who had a house they called Bell Buoy just to the east of ours. I used to ride horses when there was only one house on Nassau Point. One! Imagine that. And it was supposed to be haunted, so we always rode quickly by.

When we were young, we played on the beach. When we were older, we played tennis and golf, and swam and sailed. And we played tennis and golf, swam and sailed until we married husbands and wives who also played tennis and golf, and swam and sailed. It was just the most easy life as I look at it now. But privileged? I suppose it was in terms of what people have now. But we only had three or four servants and I had cousins who had 27! We didn't seem to have that much money. It just seemed to us an average life.

People in those days, whether they were little people or grown people, all went to picnics on the beach. And conversation, in the sense that it does not exist any longer, was the main thing. What do I mean? Well, people do not talk interestingly anymore. You know what they say about conversation . . . Stupid people talk about things. Medium people talk about people. Intelligent people talk about ideas. If you notice, this is true.

How has it changed out here? Oh honey, you know how things change. There were very few houses and each of them had acres and acres around them. I have a house in Vermont. It's not a home because I can't live there in the winter. It has no heat. But my house in Vermont is very much like Peconic used to be 50 years ago. You know, few people, very simple ways.

I was here during the hurricane of '38 with my two small children. I set them to whitening their shoes to keep them occupied while I hammered blankets over the windows. I'm afraid I wasn't quite up to the job. My training had not prepared me for practical things . . . Well, three days later when I tried to take them down, I couldn't. Those nails were really hammered in!

My childhood home in the city was five stories high and it was well staffed. Besides two or three live-in people, we had a man who came to do the heavy cleaning, a laundress who came every day, a manicurist who came once a week, and then there were the seamstresses who came to make my mother's dresses — I can remember her being fitted in a lovely grey silvery silk . . .

My father was a doctor, a heart and lung specialist, and I could see that he worked very hard. In those days doctors would go out at night to make house calls and whatever. He actually died on the job during the flu epidemic of 1918. He was taking care of his patients and he got the flu and died.

My mother had already passed on. She died during an operation when I was only eight. The thing I know about it is that she stayed in town and my sister and I were sent away to an aunt's in Westchester where we stayed knowing that something was wrong with mother, but not knowing exactly what . . . And one morning, it turned out it was the morning of the operation, I suddenly said, "I want to go to New York. I must go to New York." Had to go. Must go. And they said, no, impossible, and this must have been the time of the operation. I remember going upstairs, the maid had opened the bed and it was a bare spring, and I threw myself across it and cried for three hours. I have a certain amount of ESP and this was just the time that she was dying.

After mother died, a nurse was, of course, essential. Ours was named Clara, but we called her Caie, and she stayed with us all the while we were growing up and until she, too, passed away. When we went away for weekends Caie went with us as a chaperone. Darling, I wasn't allowed to go to the theater with my cousin without a chaperone. And I was already 18! It was quite a different world in that respect. But it was a beautiful world; I don't think that my grandmother would have admitted that any of the ugly things we now see in the newspapers or on television even existed. I still won't have a television. It's too noisy. Too bothering.

I went to Vassar, and worked on the Vassar *Miscellany News* and after that I had a fellowship in playwriting to Harvard. I later did some of that and also some design work with Norman BelGeddes — you name it, I've done it. But what turned out to be the most profitable way of writing, as I suppose it still is, was advertising copy. I did that for a number of years.

My future plans? I hope I'll die, Lord God! This is something I never thought about. About dwindling and having things go wrong and having difficulty getting up stairs. It does not seem to me that people who are not useful, who are not able to contribute to the lives of anyone, should continue taking dollars and cents and doctor's care.

I have friends who believe quite seriously in God. My grandfather was an Episcopalian minister. But I have no firm belief, though it would be very comfortable to have one. I mean, it would be nice to think that I could have another incarnation or another try at the whole bit. What would I like to come back as? I have a friend who says she'd like to come back as a bird. But I can't imagine being anyone but myself — only doing it better.

— *June 23, 1983*

Bill Dugan

Bill Dugan

*"I want to tell you about Reeves Park," said the voice on
the telephone. The caller was Bill Dugan, a long-time
"summer person," who said he had a story to tell about
the area, the people and old times in the popular
Riverhead bungalow colony located close to Long Island
Sound. What follows is a compilation of over 40 years of
memories which began even before the first bungalow was
built on the now densely-populated, 85-acre property.*

We came out here in 1942 with our
two-year-old son. That was when we
bought the bungalow, but before
that we used to camp here at the head
of the road. The property was owned by a Mr. O'Brien
at that time and he allowed us to pitch a tent and stay
all summer. So that's how we got our start as summer
residents in Reeves Park.

Reeves Park started out with two men who were

partners, a Mr. Griffing and Mr. O'Brien. They bought up 85 acres of land out here and later on they had a disagreement, so they split the property in two, with each taking a side. It was almost like the Hatfields and the McCoys. People would ask you where you lived and you'd say, "Oh, I live on the Griffing side or I'm on O'Brien's side."

Now Mr. Griffing was a real on-going person. He wanted to make money so he built up his side of the property with proper roads and then he started to put in bungalows. Mr. O'Brien took this more as a hobby, at least it seemed that way to me, because he allowed us to camp out there and store our equipment in his barn over the winter.

We were coming out here for about three years and by then Mr. O'Brien had built a few bungalows, I think there were 13 of them at the time, and my sister bought one. Then her husband went into the service, it was wartime, and she couldn't carry it, so we decided to buy it.

You know how we bought this place? There were no survey maps. O'Brien and I came out here and he said you own the property and the bungalow up to this tree and out to the rock in back. Then we went down to the local bar and he tells me the price is $1,350. So I told him I wasn't in any position to give him more than a small down payment, and he says that's OK, you pay me $15 a month — no interest — and we had a drink together, shook hands and we were in business.

It took me seven years to pay off the debt. At the time Mr. O'Brien supplied us with water for $12 a year and the taxes were $30 annually. Now they're almost $1,000 and our water bill turns $212 — and that's for Temik water. We're now paying more per year than we paid for the whole place — and it came furnished!

My family came from the Red Hook section of Brooklyn and to us Long Island really seemed like the country. Not to make a biography out of this, but my father was a painter in the shipyards and we lived with my grandfather in an apartment. My mother had three boys who were Dugans. Then my father died when I was one and she remarried and had three daughters with my stepfather, who I called "pop." My stepfather was one of the most wonderful people that anyone would ever meet. We lived a real family life. This is what is so interesting to me because I don't see any of it anymore. Pop had a car and he would load all of us, and a tent and a boat into it, and we would go off camping on the beaches from Deer Park to Wildwood. That's how we'd spend the summer. We really had a ball and we were brought up to be very self-sufficient.

We weren't exactly poor, let's just say we were struggling. By the time my wife, Virginia, and I bought the bungalow it really felt like we were upgrading ourselves.

I was a welding instructor in the navy yard when we bought this place. Before that I had worked in a sheltered workshop both as a teacher and an employee. I've got osteomyelitis and I've got a stiff leg because of it, but working in the workshop made me feel that there was nothing wrong with me. When you work with people who are far worse off than you are you don't take time to dwell on your own problems.

Our bungalow was at the end of the road. From here on there were trees. Now just look at this place. Once O'Brien got started expanding, he just couldn't stop! We'd come out in the summer and find a whole bunch of new houses had gone up. But it hasn't cramped our style, having so many more people come. We've just made more friends. We have a real community. I think there's 400 property owners here now. Those of us on the O'Brien side all chip in to maintain the roads. Nobody knows who owns them — it used to be that Mr. O'Brien maintained them. He'd come out and if he saw a pothole he'd get out his tar pot and a ladle and fill it himself. We've never received anything from the town. We have no garbage collection or hydrants and I think if we've used the fire department twice in 41 years it would be a lot. We're self-sufficient. I shouldn't say the Town has never given us anything — we do have lifeguards down at the beach.

In the old days we used to have seven or eight people packed in here every weekend. We were one big family, and if we wanted to have a party or something, we would ride around the neighborhood and yell for people to come over. It was a community thing. The bakery trucks from Dugan's and Krug's used to come through selling cake and the boy on the Dugan's truck would always yell out, "Hey boss, what'll it be today?"

It takes a long time to become accepted around here by the local people. I remember one time, many years ago, we were all at Kitinsky's — it's Bernie's Bar now — and this farmer friend of ours gets up on a stool and says, "We are all going to declare the Dugans natives!" That was really great, and I'll never forget it.

The only hardship we have out here now is the water and the taxes. We have no drinking water. The stuff in our faucets is full of Temik. I called up one of the scientists who supposedly knows all about it and he told me that the whole thing's been blown out of proportion. "Anybody can drink that water," he tells me. "I'll even come down anytime and drink it right in front of you."

OK, I told him, but would you mind putting it in writing? Oh, no, he says, he wouldn't go so far as to do that . . . These days you don't invite people in for coffee, you invite them in for a glass of pure water or for a gin and Temik.

I made one extension on this bungalow and I did all the work myself. See this floor? It cost me $7. I went to a flooring store and they had a lot of tiles left over so I bought them. There's five kinds of tiles in it, but it's pretty, don't you think? And the paneling in the bedrooms, I paid $3.50 a section for it. You couldn't do it today. So that's what I did to the place and now I'm paying for it in taxes.

I guess that's what I'm trying to say. We never bought the bungalow or worked on it with an eye towards financial gain. We did it so we'd have a place to raise our son and to have somewhere to go out of the City. It's really a shame, with the taxes and the cost of living, I don't see any young couple being able to do what we did. Even with the relative salaries, they just can't afford a nice little summer place like this one . . . It just doesn't seem fair.

— *July 21, 1983*

Edward and Jessie Schurmann

Edward and Jessie Schurmann

Bronx residents Edward and Jessie Schurmann have been summer people in Orient for over 50 years. In May of 1983 they celebrated their 60th wedding anniversary. Mr. Schurmann is 90 years old and his wife is 84. They are the parents of one child, and have three grandchildren and eight great-grandchildren. The Schurmanns were interviewed at the cottage where they have spent so many summers, near the water's edge in Orient.

Edward: My wife Jessie and I have been coming out to Orient for 40 — no, 50 years. We first came out here when our daughter, Edna, was just a young girl.
Jessie: We always went to New Jersey, but my bro-ther-in-law said to us one particular weekend, "I'm tired of New Jersey, let's go to Long Island for a change."

Edward: We stopped at the Booth House, in Greenport, and they had no accommodations so the owner called up the Orient Point Inn and they said come on over. We started out to do just that, but we came to the monument on the Lane in Orient, and we saw a big sign, "Bay House Cottages." So we came down here to have a look. It was a beautiful place, and we never did get to the Orient Point Inn. We rented a room here right away. I guess you could say we got here just by luck, and we've been coming out here ever since.

Jessie: Orient was exactly the same then as it is now.

Edward: That's right. It wasn't much different 50 years ago than it is today. You make that turn at the monument and everything looks exactly the same as it always did.

Jessie: This cottage we stay in now was once five separate rooms. In fact, our bedroom is the very first room we stayed in when we first came out here. It is kind of a change to go back to the Bronx at the end of the summer, but it's not so bad. We've lived in the same apartment there for over 40 years.

Edward: We live in the upper Bronx, near Wood-lawn. I've lived in the Bronx all my life and so has my wife. When I was a boy there was a farm in back of where we lived. My mother used to send me with a can to get milk from the farmer's cow.

Orient is really a very quiet town. You hear sometimes about people complaining about the noise of cars going by. Where we live in the Bronx the cars go by all night long. When the fire apparatus goes by I don't even wake up.

Sometimes there's a little noise from a party at the

yacht club, but we never joined it. It's for the elite. I shouldn't say the elite . . . It's for those people with houses up on the hill — the people who have boats and have children who have boats.

When we first started coming out here there were just a few cars — Tin Lizzies, we called 'em. Wagons used to come down to the potato barn at the end of the pier where the yacht club is now. They'd bag 'em there and the oyster boat would take them away. We used to have all the potatoes we wanted — right off the road.

You've heard 'em talk about the Great Depression? Well all those mansions up on the hill were for sale at that time. We used to go up there and roam around. In those days you could buy a house in the village for a song. I never did. I never had enough money to have a summer home.

Jessie: Besides, he didn't want one. He said he worked hard enough all year round. He didn't want to spend his vacation working on another home.

Edward: You didn't get long vacations in those days . . . I was never a rich man, but I made a fairly good salary — a little better than the average factory worker or what have you. I was a photoengraver. It was an interesting line of work because the technology graduated from black and white to what they called gravure, which was in brown. Then we went into color. The first color photo we made was of Santa Claus and he came out with green whiskers! We didn't know what we were doing. Today, you look in magazines and it's unbelievable, the color you see.

Jessie: We came out here during the war years. I remember one night we must have had 65 people in the Bay House, all playing cards by candlelight.

Edward: That was during the blackouts. The

An Oral History of the North Fork   91

causeway was patrolled by the army. There was no lights out there at all. You weren't allowed to turn your car headlights on. Somebody would have to walk in front of your car to guide it. You can imagine what it was like going along the causeway on a dark night.

I'll be 91 in September. How I've managed to live so long I couldn't say. I never was into health food and I think this vitamin business is all baloney. We drink a cocktail before dinner.

Jessie: I don't smoke, but he smokes cigars.

Edward: I smoke cigars morning till night.

Jessie: You can tell. My curtains are a mess from all his smoke. But we get along. He's a good husband. Of course, he had a good wife. We met when I was 18, but we didn't get married until I was 23 and Ed was 30. We were married on May 25, 1923. It was on a Friday and we were married at my mother's house.

Edward: They didn't have those big blowouts like they have today.

Jessie: We had dinner at home with the family — it was a big spread. Afterwards, I said let's get a taxi, and Ed says, a taxi? What for? We only live a few blocks from here and I want some fresh air. On my wedding night he wanted me to walk home! You should have heard my family yell at him. You oughta be ashamed of yourself, they told him.

Edward: Previous to getting married we had hired a three room apartment and furnished it with plans of getting married and living in it.

Jessie: From that time on we've lived pretty good. "Course, we have our scraps now and then, but that goes with it. We're doing pretty good and I hope the Good Lord spares us some more. We enjoy life. We really do.

— *August 11, 1983*

Up-Lot Reveries

Iola Adams

Iola Adams

Iola Adams, 87, first came to the North Fork nearly a half-century ago. Impressed by the area's beauty and rich history, and by "working and saving, saving all the time," she and her husband, James, eventually were able to purchase property and a home in Cutchogue, where she now resides. A former historian for the Southold American Legion, Mrs. Adams spent most of her life as a housekeeper and cook in private homes in New York City.

I tell you, I'm kind of surprised you wanted to meet me. I don't have much to say — I'm kind of on the quiet side. I mean to be friendly but, you know, I just can't blurt in on people. Way back when I came up, you weren't allowed to do those things.

I was born Aug. 24, 1896, in Greensboro, N. C. That's the first thing by grandmother ever taught me when I was old enough to talk. She had my birthday written in her bible and it was important to her that I knew it. My grandmother was never a field-hand. That makes a difference in the culture of children. She was a midwife and she was owned by the Wheelers. They used to call her Aunt Nancy, and she was like the mother of the whole caboodle of 'em. Mr. Wheeler was best friends with Sam Houston. I remember my grandmother used to take me up to the Wheeler Plantation near High Point. After I was nine years old, she didn't take me up there anymore. There was too much worry about what they called "intermingling." That's about all I remember about Greensboro.

From there we moved to Norfolk. My father was a veterinarian's assistant and he traveled all over the world with the race horses. Then we moved to Baltimore, because Baltimore had the Pimlico Race-track. I began working as a housekeeper in Baltimore when I was 12 years old. Back in those days children worked. We didn't sit around like these kids now. The lady I worked for taught me everything I know about cooking. She used to say to me, "Oli" — she never called me Iola, — "Oli, you're a nice girl. You hold your head high!" I must say, she gave me a good background. I worked for her during the summer and in the other months I went to school. My mother was in the first graduating class of A and M College in Greensboro and she sent me to a private Presbyterian school. I didn't know what public school was.

The woman I worked for, one of her daughters sang in the Metrolitan Opera. After I was married, I came up north to work for her in Garden City. I was making $2 a week doing housework in Baltimore and that's why I came up here, to make more money. That was the year that Harding was elected and I remember all the big fancy stores in New York had models of Mrs. Harding's inaugural gown in the windows.

I was married in 1916 . . . or was it 17? . . . I can never remember. My husband, James Adams, was from Baltimore. We were married just before the First World War. He was in the army and we didn't know if he was coming back or not. James got shipped overseas. In those days the colored soldiers didn't do anything but stevedore work.

How did he feel about that? Back in those days you didn't feel any way about anything. You did what you were told to do. Just before World War II he enlisted again in the National Guard and he was in the 369th Regiment as a sergeant bugler.

We had two children, but our son died. Back then they had the flu, you know, and the germ was spreading all over. I used to wash for the nurses at Johns Hopkins Hospital and I evidently brought the germ home, 'cause my baby died, but my daughter, she was older, and she didn't get it.

During World War II, I got a job cooking for Elizabeth Arden's niece over on Nassau Point. Helena Rubenstein and all those rich folks, I mean, anybody who was anybody was there. I went back and forth between Cutchogue and our apartment in Brooklyn all that summer. We never had nothing. I was saving all the time. But I'll tell you, property out here was cheap then. So we bought some — for $300 — and later we got a mortgage to build a house, which we built ourselves.

Meanwhile, I began working for a doctor in New York City. I always stayed a long time on my jobs and I only went to the agency once. I always worked in

New York 'cause you could make more money. You could get $80 or $100 a month if you were a good cook. I remember when my daughter was gong to school she used to always ask me why she didn't have any sisters or brothers like all the other families with eight or ten kids all over the place. But I *worked*, you see. We lived in our apartment in Brooklyn but we came out here on the holidays and we'd pitch a tent on our property and camp.

There were very few things I ever wanted to do or be except decent. And I'm that way today. I'm very interested in history and I was the historian for the Southold American Legion. I love old things. When we first came out here we had a police dog and she died, so my husband, he was digging her grave out in back and he found a bow and arrow.

There's a lovely group of people out here and I think the elderly people here are just gorgeous! I think it would have been nice to belong to the 18th century. I was born after freedom. I don't get the same feeling that some people get about being colored and this and that. The only thing I don't like is being called black. I like Afro-American better.

My daughter died several years ago and my husband passed away two years back, so I'm pretty much alone. I never get lonely, though. I don't know why, exactly. I don't say it's 'cause I'm so strong — but I like people; you see, if you don't like people, it's very hard to get along. I like anybody. All I ask for in return is respect.

— *September 8, 1983*

Up-Lot Reveries

Timothy G. Griffing

Timothy G. Griffing

Timothy Griffing was born in Riverhead in 1905, and is the co-founder of Griffing Hardware on West Main Street. His grandfather, Timothy M. Griffing, is remembered in the town for having built the Riverhead Water Works Tower and as the man who created Grangebel Park. A popular figure, Mr. Griffing was interviewed shortly before he was to serve as Grand Marshal of the 1983 Riverhead Country Fair Parade.

Being chosen Grand Marshal of the parade was the farthest thing from my mind. I told the Town Supervisor that I couldn't walk it. I'm still a fireman, but I haven't marched in any parade in the last two or three months 'cause my legs won't take it. At first they were going to have an open car, but now I understand there's going to be an open buggy. That'll be nice because I used to drive around in a surrey with the fringe on top.

I was born and brought up in Riverhead across from where Griffing Hardware now stands. My birthday was April 9, 1905. I was born in a little house that didn't have electricity or running water; we had a hand pump. Later, my parents built a bigger house next door to it. I remember when they were building our new house my mother tied me to the grape arbor on a clothesline that would just not let me get in the way of the builders. When we moved into our new house my parents asked me what I missed most about our old house and what do you suppose I told them? The pump! I guess I pumped a lot of water for my mother. Those were the days . . .

Main Street was a dirt road when I was a boy. The cars got thicker and thicker as years went on. I went to school at the old wooden school building on Roanoke Avenue, which has since burned down. We used to ride down the street in a car and there was still a drinking fountain at the intersection of Peconic Avenue and Main Street. The pace of life in those days was different. People didn't hurry. There was always something to do, though. Never a dull moment.

Timothy M. Griffing was my grandfather. He died in 1924, so I grew up knowing him. He was a stern individual and yet a nice, shall we say, old man, because I remember him as an old man. He was a lawyer and a county judge of Suffolk County for eight years. Of course, everyone remembers him as the man who built the famous Riverhead Water Works Tower that supplied the village with water for years. Nine people out of 10 thought that the tower was

Up-Lot Reveries

made of stone, but it wasn't. It was made of wood. It was designed after a castle someplace. I've forgotten where. It was something my grandfather saw and wanted copied. He and grandmother went abroad a lot. The first floor of the tower was a grist mill and second and third was where they milled flour. I can remember the farmers bringing their corn on the cob and we'd run it through the grinding machine and it came out as feed for the cattle. My father ran the feed and grist mill for several years. We put up flour in barrels under the Ceresota brand. There was a searchlight on top of the tower that my father would turn on at night to help guide the boatmen up the river. When the water company was dissolved and they built the water tower Riverhead uses now, we used to keep a little water in the tower for the gardens. The tank took up the fourth and fifth floors of the tower. There was an elevator up to the third floor, but from there you had to take the stairs. I can remember going up to the fifth floor and there used to be a ladder down into the tank and in the winter we'd ice skate on it. The pump house for the water tower still stands in Grangebel Park. It's the little brick building just off Peconic Avenue. They took the tower down in 1948. It got to be unsafe. The underpinnings were rotting out. Too bad, it was quite a showpiece.

Grandfather named Grangebel Park after his three daughters, Grace, Angeline and Mabel. They were very nice ladies. There was a lily pond in back of where the European American Bank is now that was stocked with goldfish and my grandparents' house stood nearby. We had a pony at my grandfather's barn. He also had a horse, two cows and a couple of automobiles. One was a chain drive locomobile that had a pan underneath it to catch the drippings. One day the hired man had this pan off alongside the car. I was over at the particular time wearing a chinchilla coat and I got too close to the pan and fell over into it backwards! I don't remember exactly what my mother said, but I do remember that grease all over my chinchilla coat.

A few years ago I changed cars. After 14 Fords, I decided. All my life I wanted a Cadillac and we finally go it. My first Ford was a Model T Roadster with wooden spoked wheels. I bought if from a Polish man and I remember he said to me at the time, "Now, remember, this a yank 'em car. No self-commencer." He meant you had to crank it. There was no self-starter. No self-commencer.

I majored in business administration at Rider College in Trenton, N.J. I had started out in engineering at Cornell and I soon found out, because calculus and physics busted me, that that wasn't what I wanted to do.

My brother and I opened Griffing Hardware on Oct. 26, 1931. I've been behind that counter for 52 years. There are three generations of us working there now. We have a pretty good reputation that if you want to find something, go to Griffings. We started out with a small store. It is the east half of what is now E.F. Hutton. My father helped us build the present store where we are now. We've been in there since 1933.

My wife just had her 80th birthday. The children and the grandchildren gave her a weekend in New York City, which included me, of course. Her maiden name was Alice Bradford Terrell. We were married on June 30, 1928, in a double wedding. My wife's sister was also married during the ceremony to my fourth cousin, William Sweezey Conklin. It was at 12:30 at the Methodist Church in Riverhead. There was a big to-do afterwards at the house my wife and I lived in for 35 years on Second Street, across from the post office. There was a reception and a caterer came out from New York City with five truckloads of supplies. There were 100 invited guests and 24 in the wedding party. We took moving pictures during the ceremony and I still have the film. We show it every now and then and everyone has a good laugh. Strange though, every time we watch it we see someone else who's passed away. That's just the way life is, I guess.

We have quite a family. Five children, 10 grandchildren and three great-grandchildren. Alice and I have been married for 55 years. It doesn't seem that long.

Up until a few years ago I used to have long sideburns, mutton chops they called 'em, and a mustache that I copied after my grandfather. I grew them for a beard-growing contest and I won first prize. Now with the Country Fair and the parade and everything, I guess I'll have to get ahold of Benny Poudel to see if he can paste whiskers on my face.

The unhurried pace of the good old days makes for fond memories, but the recent changes I've seen in this town have mostly all been for the better. I think Riverhead's headed in the right direction.

— *September 29, 1983*

Carl Vail

Carl Vail

*Carl Vail, 88, began selling cars in Southold in 1919.
A decorated veteran of World War I, he and his wife,
Inez, have three children, eight grandchildren, and
eleven great-grandchildren.*

I was born on a farm in Peconic on Aug. 12, 1895. My parents had eight children, but one of them died in infancy. I was the youngest boy and I had two younger sisters. My father was a combination farmer and salesman. He was the first salesman to travel Long Island in a car — a 1905 Pierce Arrow Motorette. He represented a hardware firm, and I don't know if having a car helped his sales, but it sure helped him get around. It was better than a horse and wagon, even if it did only have a one-cylinder, eight-horsepower engine.

When my 50th anniversary in the automobile business came up, I had so many franchises that I couldn't pick any one to put on my anniversary plaque, so I chose the old Pierce Arrow. I even had a cut of it engraved on our gravestones in the old cemetery in Cutchogue.

I learned to drive on that car in 1908 when I was 13 years old. We had gone up to west Mattituck. There was a school on the dip on the hill and that's where we were standing when the last Vanderbilt Cup Race came through Mattituck. The car that was favored to win, an Apperson Jackrabbit, hit a patch of sand right in front of us and overturned into a ditch. The driver survived but his mechanic was killed. The sight and shock of that smash-up was unforgettable. I've been preaching and practicing highway safety ever since.

Anyway, on the way home my father let me drive the car. Was I scared? Well, there was no traffic and the car was very simple. Its top speed was only about 25 miles an hour — fast for those days, but not fast enough for us kids. My older sister, Alicia, had a boyfriend with a really fast trottin' horse and it could go right past us! That didn't go over too good and we hoped that when father got another car it would at least beat Sister's boyfriend's horse, and it did.

He got a Haynes-Apperson. That car had a two-cylinder engine, a very short wheel base and lots of bad habits. It had a planetary transmission, like the old Fords had, and sometimes when you got it in gear it stuck. When father would take us for a ride, one of us kids would be delegated to throw the switch in order to cut the motor if he couldn't get it out of gear . . .

We had a cauliflower barn at our home, and of course a cauliflower barn, you could drive a team of horses right through it. There were big doors on each end of the thing. So one day we was out riding in the

Up-Lot Reveries

car and my sister, who had the assignment of turning off the switch, failed to do so soon enough and we all went sailing right in through the open front doors of the cauliflower barn and out the back, which was closed!

Then the darn thing had a habit of when you got it up to about 35 miles an hour somewhere along the line a spring would lock the steerin' arm and it would take you right off the road . . . That car didn't stay in the family too long.

The next car we got was a 1914 four cylinder Buick and that was a good car. After that, we got a Franklin air-cooled and that was a great car . . . I guess it's true, I do have a tendency to remember things in terms of cars.

I was runnin' the farm fairly successfully, just before World War I broke out. I had 3,000 chickens and several cows. Then the war came along and I figured I owed it to my country to get into the service. I tried to get into the Navy because I like the water, but the only opening they had was for a ship's cook. So they gave me an examination for that job, and due to the fact that we had a steam canner at home, I just guessed the time to cook meats and so forth in a pressure cooker and they said, OK, you can go in as a cook. But I didn't really want to be a cook, so I said no and notified the draft board to forget my agricultural exemption and put me in the Army.

I went to Camp Upton on Dec. 5, 1917 — the coldest winter in my memory. It was down to 17 below zero and they didn't have anything but campaign hats for us and no shoes to fit me. You know, when it's really cold like that you don't like to talk, so the officers would say, "Now, when we go out to drill if you get one pat on the back your ears are freezing. If you get two pats you're excused to go back to the barracks to thaw out." That darn barracks was built by a lot of make-shift carpenters and when it snowed, why it had a ventilator that would fill up and then send all the melted water down on the beds. In those days anybody who had any lousy coal to sell sold it to the government, so when you washed your socks and hung them up to dry around the stove, why they'd freeze right fast . . . It was a great place. I was there from Dec. 5 until sometime in April when we shipped off to France.

I was taken off the ship in England with a case of German measles and sent to a hospital. Then I got over that and was on my way to Winchester when I came down with scarlet fever. So I was sent to another hospital near Winchester and what a place that was. It almost seemed that you had to get everything that was going around there before you could get out. I had acute Bright's disease there and bronchitis and they finally cut my tonsils out. The doctor who operated on me had accidentally cut a fella's jugular vein the day before. What's worse, the captain assigned to the hospital was stealin' the ration money and we were starved. The nurses were even bringing us bread crusts from their tables. If I'd have met the guy who was in charge of that place, why, I'd of been up for murder. Fortunately, I didn't meet up with him . . .

I was hospitalized from April until August and when the Germans got pretty well near Paris they took everybody that didn't have a fever out of every hospital. I'd been in a bed, flat on my back for three weeks and zip — I was headed for the front. It took me five days travelin' around France to find my division.

Up-Lot Reveries

Nobody knew where it was, but each main city had an American dispatch office and I had open travel orders, so I'd walk in and say, "I want to get back to the 77th Division," and they'd say, "Well, I think they're so and so." So I'd take the name of the city and get on the next transportation. One day I got on a freight train with a bunch of Senegalese troops — you know those guys was seven feet tall and they used to crawl over the lines with bowie knives in their teeth. Well, they damn sure showed me quick that they didn't want me with 'em, and I managed to get out right fast.

I was on the trains for five days and five nights before I finally reached my division, which was on its way to changin' fronts. I musta walked a mile with my pack and it weighed 100 pounds before I told the captain, "God, I can't go any further." So he says, "Where you been the last three weeks," And I tell him flat on my back in the hospital. "Oh," he says, "You had a nice rest."

The first night on the front I dug into a foxhole on a side hill and the Germans shelled the hell out of it and started a landslide. Buried me alive — my buddies dug me out before I suffocated. I musta been fast asleep when the shell struck. When they dug me out my knees were banging together and I couldn't do anything about it. I concentrated and thought, my God, what a hell of a soldier you are. And I concentrated and gritted my teeth and finally my knees stopped shakin'. Later on I had a reputation in the company for not being afraid of anything. But they didn't know . . .

Having been brought up in the country I knew my directions pretty well so they made me a runner and guide. When all the communications was shot up as they generally were in a barrage, they sent me out.

The first time I went out I didn't know which way the shells was going. I was literally blown from one shell hole to another — and some of them damn shell holes was 30 feet deep. But I got there and back without a scratch . . . I'd made up my mind very early in my experiences that if the Germans was going to get me they were going to have to get me on the run, not settin' still like a settin' duck. So anything that came up, I volunteered. I got all kinds of jobs. One of the biggest things, you know, was that I couldn't bear to see my buddies bleed to death, so I volunteered to carry the front end of the stretcher anytime any of them got wounded. I guess you could say that I recuperated from my hospital experiences very quickly once I reached the front, but I always had a tough constitution, I think. Back in Southold High School I was a halfback on the football team and a center on the basketball team. I was a pretty rugged farmer in those days.

I was in France for a year and then I went back to the states. I'll tell you, that Statue of Liberty was one welcome sight.

Right now I'm strugglin' with reports of my activities overseas because Congressman Carney has a good share of my records and I'm being considered for a Congressional Medal of Honor. I already got a Purple Heart — but I didn't get it until last year. That was after I joined The World War I Barrracks, a veteran's organization, about two years ago. There's a man there, Marion Pond's his name, and he's the adjutant of the barracks. Anyways, one day he says to us that his job was to get us all the medals we deserved. And he asks me, "What've you got?" And I tell him, "Nothing." So he asks me, "Did you keep a diary?" and

I says yes, so he asks me to let him read it. Then he comes back and he says, "My God, you not only deserve a Purple Heart, you did more than enough to rate a Congressional Medal of Honor," and he's been working on it ever since.

When I got back to the states from France I decided to go back to Cornell and finish up my college education. So I went up there to make up third year German and, lo and behold, I commenced to lose a pound a day! So the Veteran's Bureau called me in for an examination and they says, "You can't concentrate after what you've been through — you have to quit." Then they said I shouldn't do anything for three years. Well, I couldn't stand that. I tried it, but finally I said to my father, "Gee, my brother's a good mechanic and you're a good salesman, let's go to New York and get an automobile franchise. Maybe I can ride around in an open car and get my health back." So we went to New York and, of course, it was after the war and nothing was available that was worth a darn. Then, while we were driving back through Brooklyn we saw a whole lot full of beautiful blue touring cars. Metz Master-Sixes they were — war babies, made in Waltham, Mass. We bought one of them outright and put down a $500 deposit on two more. See, we was green as grass. It took one whole year to sell those three cars. We changed the name of 'em at least in our minds, from Metz Master-Six to Metz Nasty-Six, because after they'd been run 2,000 miles the piston would come up above the block and catch the rings and break the top of the piston off. I just went to see Steve Doroski in Southold the other day and his father-in-law, Adam Zaveski, bought the first one of those cars from me and I taught him how to drive it. 'Course, we weren't making a very good livin', with those Metz Masters, so we sold Fords for a man named H. E. Campbell and he used to give $25 for each car we sold plus we had to teach the new owners how to drive. Then we sold Overlands for Fred Jennings in Southold, and we sold so many of them in three months that we saved enough to buy our own demonstrator. That was my start in the automobile business.

In 1927, my brother Richard and I built the garage and showroom where Wells Pontiac is now in Peconic. As better franchises became available, well we had such a good sales record that we could get them. Over the years we had over 20 different ones, but we didn't get General Motors until 1933. That's when we opened Vail Motors in Riverhead. The Peconic place was called Vail Brothers Inc., and we had a place in Southampton called Sea Vail Motors.

But we started in sellin' cars house to house. I knew every house and everybody from Baiting Hollow to Orient on the North Road, and 'most everybody on the south. I knew their names and their wives' names and sometimes their kids. I worked nights and Sundays and taught hundreds of people how to drive. I wore out my knees chasin' prospects. To add a little humor to my sales pitch, I'd say that I wore out my knees chasin' women to sell them cars. But that's how I built up the business.

Over the years I sold approximately 50,000 cars and some of my friends tell me I'm partly responsible for all the damn traffic around here. And I say, now, look. Let's examine the other side of this thing. When I first started sellin' cars I started down in Orient where everybody was cousins and I had to teach them how to drive and that permitted them to get out and circulate.

So I feel that what I did, if anything, was to save the East End of Long Island from a severe case of in-breedin.'

— October 27, 1983

Dr. Vincent Doroszka

Dr. Vincent Doroszka

Dr. Vincent Doroszka, 81, began practicing medicine in Riverhead in 1931. A short time later he bought the 14-room, turn-of-the-century Victorian home on East Main Street where he had lived and maintained an office for the past 51 years. A family physician, Dr. Doroszka was associated with Southampton Hospital as a physician and surgeon until 1950. He then became affiliated with Central Suffolk Hospital in Riverhead, where he remains as an honorary staff member. Retired since 1979, Dr. Doroszka is married to the former Arlene Ostroski of South Jamesport.

I started practicing medicine in Riverhead 51 years ago today on Dec. 8, 1931. When I first started I got $2 for an office call, $3 for a house call. I made hundreds of them at all hours of the day and night. Mostly at night, they'd call you. I delivered babies for $35. And most of them were home deliveries. They thought if you went to the hospital you were going to die. They were all delivered at home, thank-you, and I never lost a baby. Here, look at this article from the *Brooklyn Times Union* in 1935.

BABY BORN 'DEAD' NORMAL
IN TWO WEEKS

Riverhead — March 2. John Palembas Jr., who was believed to be dead when he was born two weeks ago, is now as normal as the average baby.

Dr. Vincent Doroszka of Riverhead, who attended Mrs. Mary Palembas at the birth, was unable to detect the slightest sign of life. After he had administered adrenalin and used the mouth-to-mouth method of respiration for more than an hour-and-a-half, the baby's heart began to beat normally. John Jr. was born at the home of Mrs. M. Latchick, mother of Mrs. Palembas, in Cutchogue. Mr. and Mrs. Palembas reside in Baiting Hollow. The mother was 19.

I remember it just like it was yesterday. The baby started showing slight signs of life after about 15 minutes of mouth-to-mouth resuscitation. What kept me trying? . . . Ha! I was the type who would never give up. I felt better than that mother did, I think, when I saw that baby start to breathe.

They're doing a lot of caesareans now because you're likely to lose a baby and then somebody says, hey, why didn't you do a caesarean? These hungry lawyers do that, and there's a half-million lawyers in America. There's going to be a million of them here by 1990. Now, in the Yale Medical School, which I attended, they give you law school besides, if you want it. So when you graduate you're a doctor and a lawyer as well. I approve of that wholeheartedly. Then you can give those lawyers a hard time. Lawyers are the biggest culprits in the world. Rip-off artists! Have I ever been sued? Never! I was what they call "naked" — I had no insurance for the last five years I was practicing. Who's going to sue me? I'm not doing surgery anymore. I'm not handling serious cases.

I am and was a family physician. A dying breed? . . . Dead! I paid $35 malpractice insurance when I started, now it's up in the thousands. Insanity! There's no family touch anymore. These new-breed doctors are entirely different. They do lab work and X-ray work and that's all they do. And then they do as much as possible to pile up the bill as high as humanly possible. But they have to, because they're afraid of lawsuits and they have to have the money to pay them. I believe we're going to revert back to the way we used to be. General medicine will come around again because these days people can't afford to go to a doctor. If you have a good relationship with your patients, they're not going to sue you.

I was born in Cutchogue on the last day of July, 1902. So therefore I am a young man yet. I was a farm boy and I didn't go to school until I was eight-years-old. I had to stay home and pick potatoes and work like a mule. I hate farming! I would tell them I wanted to be doctor just like Doctor Stevens. He practiced in Jamesport.

My father came to this country in 1870. He went back to Poland a few years later to pick up a bride —my mother. She was very much younger than him but she married him because she had to get away from what she was doing. She was a maid for the upper classes, the elite. If the madam wanted to slam her in the face, she did it. So my mother got out of there. She was 14, maybe 15, when she married my father. I don't remember him. He died of sunstroke out in the fields, 12 days before I was born.

Mark Twain said, "In the first place God made idiots; that was for practice. Then he made school boards . . . " Did you ever see a school board worth a penny? You know what they do? Nothing! My mother never went to school. She couldn't read or write. We kids taught her how. Her maiden name was Bertha Janulewicz. Later she remarried a Zaleski. I had four brothers and sisters and five stepbrothers and sisters. My oldest stepbrother was the Bishop of Lansing, Michigan.

I went to the Laurel grammar school. Then I went to John Bosco prep. They brought us up like a bunch of monks. From there I went to Villanova. I'm an associate trustee of that school now and I'm very proud of it. I went to Yale Medical School.

Things were tough when I got out of medical school. See this? This is a United States Government form for the prescription of medicinal liquor. This was during Prohibition when I wrote them. Doctors were allowed to write prescriptions for liquor and some people would just come in here and beg for it. As far as I was concerned, they didn't need it. You had to take the prescription to the drugstore to buy whiskey, or *spiritus fermenti*, as it's called on the form.

I went into the service in July of 1942. I stayed there three years and three months traveling the seas on a casualty transport submarine. Did I like it? Like hell! It was just torture. Especially that first trip. You shook all the way up and all the way down. But after you cross the ocean 10 or 12 times you don't mind.

In the army you're just a number. Everything is expendable, including people. You don't believe it? Look at the boys getting killed over there in Beirut. What for ? Why'd we go to Vietnam? What for? Because of the stupid government! Mark Twain once said that there is no native American criminal class except Congress.

I'll be living in this house 51 years this January. My wife and I, we have no family. No children, thank God! Children are a headache. That's what I tell all my relatives. Young children, young trouble. Old children, old trouble. My patients? No, I never gave them that advice. They just thought I was a young whipper-snapper farm boy who didn't know anything anyway. Some of them even told me how to practice medicine. You know what I'd tell them? Well, what medical school did YOU go to and what year did YOU graduate? Forget about it! You wanna get a headache? Be a doctor.

As you can see, my hair's not even grey yet. You wanna know how I kept it this way? I told you. Chase young women, blondes, redheads, brunettes, as long as they're pretty and fascinating. That's what keeps your hair from turning grey. Then you have bright ideas, great ideas — beautiful ideas! Who in the heck wants an old fogey running around saying, "Oh, I'm 65, I'm a senior citizen." Great golden god, shape up! Nobody should stop or retire until he's 72. Nobody. I was 79 when I retired.

Am I glad I became a doctor? Yes. I wouldn't know what else to do. I am a doctor. I earned my title and I deserve to use it. What else am I supposed to do? Go jump rope?

— December 15, 1983

Lida Rafford, R. N.

Lida Rafford, R. N.

Lida Rafford, R. N., was born in Mattituck in 1897. She received her nurse's training at Methodist Hospital in Brooklyn, where she worked for nearly 40 years, much of that time as head nurse in charge of the third floor.

When she retired in 1967, Miss Rafford returned home to Mattituck. Three years ago she began assisting at a near-by Montessori training program for pre-schoolers, where at last count she had received at least four proposals of marriage from her ardent young admirers.

I was born here, right next door in a house that's no longer standing. All this land, all the way down to the next road, was once my grandfather's property. His name was Joseph Rafferty, a good old Irish name — but my father's oldest brother, he had our name changed to Rafford.

Why? I suppose he was kidded about it. But I also heard that he was going with a girl and she didn't like the name Rafferty. So she told him she wouldn't marry him if he didn't change it. My father didn't particularly want to change his name, but he went along with it.

I had three brothers and one half-brother. My mother had been married for a short time before, but her first husband died. There were very few houses or people around here when I was growing up. Out the window here, where all the houses are, was once all meadow grass. I was down here with no kids to play with except my brothers and the neighbor boys . . . What was that like? I loved it! I was a regular tomboy. My brother that was next in age to me — Charles, his name was — he never knew whether he had a clean pair of pants to put on or not because I was always swiping them to go climb trees.

My father had died when I was only two. So my mother was widowed twice and the second time she was left with five children to raise. Still, she managed to live to be 76. I'm older than anybody in my family ever lived to be. I'm 86 now. I was born on Oct. 19, 1897.

My mother took in washing and anything else she could do to survive. She raised chickens so that we had a chicken to eat now and then. I don't remember too much about that . . . you ate what was put before you and didn't make a fuss.

My grandfather had come here from London when my father was just five, but he was Irish through and through. The wife that he had at that time, she died in

Up-Lot Reveries

childbirth here in Mattituck. It would have been her fifth child. She died during the delivery and the baby died five days later.

Then my grandfather married my grandma, Grandma Anne, we called her. She was a comparatively young woman when she came over to marry grandpa and she was quite a character, but she did a lot of good.

She had no fear of contagion and people were always calling on her to take care of their sick children. She was very careful and when she would go into a home where there was sickness she would practically live in the room with the sick child so that nobody else got it. She did everything, from giving medicine to taking care of the wash. She hadn't studied medicine, she just had the instinct. And she was very much loved by a lot of people.

Jim Gildersleeve, he and his brothers had a store in Mattituck and every week they had a man come and get a list of whatever grandma needed and the next day they would bring the order. I don't think she ever paid for any of those groceries. Not from the things I heard her say about how good the Gildersleeves, especially Jim, were to her. Apparently, the Gildersleeve children had been very sick at one time and she had stuck with them. She was so enthusiastic about what she did that I think she influenced me, unconsciously at least, into choosing nursing as my career.

I went to Methodist Hospital in Brooklyn for my nurse's training. At first it seemed like another world. But so many of the girls there were in the same boat I was — country girls who'd had to work to earn the money to go there. In the mornings we worked on the wards with the patients and in the afternoon we went to school. We worked hard — very, very hard. But it was good training.

In those days we didn't have penicillin and we saw a lot of people die. Children too. We had one little boy I'll never forget. He was an only child. A beautiful child, just beautiful. The mother and the father were having their troubles, I guess. Anyway, the little boy was about two-and-a-half and he had bronchitis from time to time . . . One day the father went away on a business trip and when he came back he found the child alone in his crib, a mess, no food, sour milk in his nursery bottle. She gave him a nursery bottle, I think, to keep him in his crib. When the father found him he already had bronchitis and then went into pneumonia. The father rushed him to the hospital, but it went fast and furious. I stayed with him until he died. He needed a mother. He hadn't had one for a long time, apparently. I can't remember his name, but oh, that little face. I was still in training and I never worked in pediatrics after that.

But I did work in obstetrics. Almost never did you lose a mother or baby in those days. I think that's because they let things run their normal course and they didn't get into the trouble they do today. If you were having a baby, you waited and the doctor waited there with you. I think the doctors and the nurses were closer then. We were all working together to try to get the patients well using very limited resources.

The doctors and the surgeons would come in to teach us. There weren't many women training to be doctors then and the ones that were they treated like dogs. Gave them all the dirty work to do. Some of them managed to succeed, though. They were tough as nails. They had to be.

Up-Lot Reveries

Nursing was depressing at times, but you know, there was a lot of joy in it too. And remember, we were very young and full of fun when we were off-duty. During training, we didn't have much money to spend, so we made our own good times. We had a piano and one of the girls played and sometimes we'd dance. I never got married, I just made nursing my life. I was at Methodist for 39-and-a-half years. I never became a nursing supervisor because I felt I could do more working with the student nurses right out on the floor — and I could, too. I was head nurse on the third floor for many, many years . . . See this? I got this note yesterday from a nurse I trained 53 years ago. Isn't that something? It's so good to hear from somebody. But how many take the time to really sit down and write?

I retired in 1967 and came back to Mattituck. A few years ago I began helping in the Montessori program. I love those children. They really are adorable and the job has really been a lifesaver for me. You know, it keeps you interested in things and in what's going on around you.

A year ago I had an operation and I swear they took out my ears and my forgettery when they did it. They're just not as good as they were before. And I've slowed down — but I don't feel 86.

My dog Heidi here has probably helped prolong my life because I've spent a good deal of time walking her. Between her and the children, they give me something to do everyday. Something to get out of bed for. I like people. I'd be lost without people. It wouldn't be a happy world without them.

— *February 9, 1984*

Marion Terry

Marion Terry

Marion Terry was born in Riverhead in 1898. Her mother, Carrie, was one of 10 children born to Emeline Aldrich Corwin and her husband, Hubbard, a Long Island Railroad employee turned farmer in Riverhead.

In 1852, Hubbard Corwin had built the two-story Italianate home known as Eastlawn on East Main Street. There he raised his family and later entertained his grandchildren, including Marion, who still has fond memories of Sunday dinners at her grandfather's house.

In 1956, Miss Marion Terry inherited Eastlawn, where she lived with her two sisters, Eva and Rose, until just a few years ago.

I saw in the papers where they called the house I used to live in the Marion Terry House. Well, that's not right. It was always known as the Corwin House. Terry never came into it. It was built by my grandfather, Hubbard

Corwin, in 1852.

We never lived in it while I was growing up. My family lived on the corner of Roanoke Avenue and Second Street. But I can remember going to my grandfather's house for Sunday dinners. When I went home they'd ask me what I had for dinner and I'd say "gravy!" Grandfather was a very nice man. By the time I knew him he was an invalid. I remember that after dinner the family would take him outside in his wheelchair and I'd stand on the steps with him. He had eight daughters and two sons. Three of his daughters never married and they stayed with him.

My grandfather worked for the Long Island Railroad for awhile. He was in charge of a train they called the Adam Express that ran between Greenport and Brooklyn. At one time they lived in Greenport, but meanwhile he owned all this land in Riverhead. It began on East Main Street and ran across the railraod tracks all the way to Middle Road. So he severed his connection with the railroad and began farming in Riverhead.

My father, Dr. Henry Parsons Terry, was a country doctor, I guess you could say. He had an office in Cutchogue before he moved to Riverhead. His first wife died, I don't know what of, soon after that move. So did his son. He marrried my mother, Carrie Corwin Terry, in 1897. She was a teacher, and I'd imagine she was in her 30s when she married him. I was their only child, but I had three half-sisters, Eva, Rose, and Heddy.

When I was a little girl my best friend lived down the street on East Main Street. Her name was Marion Howell and her older sister, Edith, is still living, I think. Marion was what you'd call a delicate child. She died in her early 20s.

Other than my best friend, I remember having dolls and a wonderful cat when I was a girl. I would walk over to Marion's house — there were lots of houses on East Main Street then. And there was a lily pond in Grangebel Park with a waterfall near the entrance.

My sister Eva went away to college and then taught school at a couple of places in New Jersey. Rose was the one that stayed at home. She worked as a secretary for one of the lawyers in town. I went to grade school in the building that stood on Roanoke Avenue. I don't remember too much about high school. I wasn't the popular type, I guess. I was what you might call a book worm. I graduated high school in 1917 and went to college at Oberlin in Ohio. Then I worked as a college librarian for many years, first in Denver, Colorado, then back east in Lancaster, Pennsylvania, and in Farmville, Virginia.

I never married and I don't think I missed anything. I can't say I ever thought much about it. I love books and I still love to read — light stuff now, mysteries and so forth.

Riverhead has changed. For the better? I don't know. I remember across from my grandfather's there was the most wonderful strawberry patch. And then there were the asparagus . . . Of course, they couldn't keep all that land so close to the business district in farms.

When my Aunt Frances died in 1956 I inherited grandfather's house. I don't think there was any question but that I would take it. I wanted it. It was the family home and I loved it. I think the family kind of expected that I would take care of it too. Anyway, I moved into it with my sisters Eva and Rose and I stayed there until Eva died several years ago. By then I couldn't keep up with it anymore.

Now I hear that they're thinking of moving it. It's a wonder they don't just tear it down. But I guess they're getting more careful about doing things like that.

I don't know what good it would do to move it though. It would be too big a change. Then again I don't know that it would appeal to anybody where it is right now. Would it?

Well, I'll let them settle that. I'm happy where I am. I can do my own shopping and have lunch out when I want it. I'm still independent. And I hope to stay that way.

— *March 8, 1984*

Mary
Fleming Mayo

Mary
Fleming Mayo

*At 84, Mary Fleming Mayo is one of the oldest of the
many members of Riverhead's black community who
trace their roots back to Powhatan, Va., a largely rural
county approximately 30 miles from the capitol of
Richmond.*

*Like most of the hundreds of people who migrated here
from Powhatan, Mrs. Mayo and her late husband,
German, came to Riverhead to work on the area's farms.
They stayed to raise a family and to play an active role in
the life of their church, Riverhead's First Baptist, where
Mrs. Mayo served as clerk for over 21 years.*

I was born on April 18, 1899, in Powhatan, Va.
That sounds like an Indian name and it could
be, 'cause my grandfather, George Fleming,
was part Indian and from the way he looked,

one of his parents must have been white. His picture is in the church that he built down there — The Shiloh Church. He was a carpenter. I was just a child when he was around.

My family's all gone from there now and that great big house we used to live in — it was built by my grandfather with two stories and two porches, one in the front and one in the back — it's gone, too. But I was raised there with nine brothers and three sisters. My father was a farmer. He grew so much corn and wheat and things that he had to take the extra in the wagon and sell it in Richmond. We never worried for a mouthful of anything, so help me God!

I didn't have to work much at home, I had too many brothers for that. But I had to sweep the yard. We didn't have rakes like they do now. I used a dogwood broom. My mama had all of her babies at home. The midwife would come and they wouldn't even let you into the house when it was going on. I know they let children see babies being born now, but I don't think they should. Their time will come when they have their own babies.

I remember we had two mules named Tom and Jerry and the horses were named Alice and Hazel and Bonnie and Maude. Daddy used a two-mule team to plow. They didn't know nothin' from tractors in those days. I didn't especially like to ride those horses, but sometimes I had to 'cause if my mother wanted to send a pail of soup or some cake or bread to someone less fortunate than we were, I'd have to get on a horse and take it to them.

I went to school in Powhatan in a one-room schoolhouse that had all the grades in together. And do you know where I got my high school education? In

Up-Lot Reveries

front of the fireplace in my mama's room!

At night, mama would make me put out the lamps so there'd be oil left in them in the morning to get up by. So, when I put the lamps out, I'd throw some kindling in the fireplace and lay down by it and study. That's how I got my high school education. Later, I went to summer classes at the Virginia Union University, but the teachers told me I knew as much as they did. So they gave me a certificate to teach and I taught in two rural school districts down there in Ballsville and Trenholm. They were both all-black schools. I don't think the children missed anything for it. I came up in an all-black school and even today I don't believe you could ask me a word I couldn't spell — and I'm in my eighties.

There's a lot of people from Powhatan here in Riverhead and I guess I'm one of the oldest. I was over 21 when I came up here. I remember because I got married — I can't remember when — it's terrible to get so senile. I wasn't like this before I had thyroid and the operation on my leg. But I remember my mother told me I could get married today or tomorrow, but I would never remember coming back in her house again. She just didn't like my husband.

So I said to her, with a smile, you know you didn't talk to your parents rude in those days, no indeed! I said well, suppose I'm married to him already? She didn't say anything, but so help me God, after I did marry him she told me that he was the only son-in-law she had! That's because he'd go out and get the water from the well for her and he'd get the wood off the woodpile. My sister's husband, he's deceased now, he'd walk right through the yard without drawing a pail of water. My husband, his name was German

Mayo, he was altogether different.

We came up to Riverhead because people here were hiring men from Virginia to work on the farms. German worked on the Goodale's farm in Aquebogue for a long, long time. I didn't think the white people would accept me as they did. Even the lady next door, when we bought this house she came over and shook my hand and said since we're neighbors, we might as well be friends. And she's been like that ever since. I have her number right by my telephone and I know if I ever have a problem, even if it's at 12 o'clock at night, she'll come right over.

My husband and I had four children — three boys and one girl. All of them went to school in Riverhead and attended church at Riverhead First Baptist — that's the church that's on the Northville Turnpike now. That church is real important to the members of this community. I served as clerk there for 21 years and four months.

None of my sons live around here anymore but my daughter Marian does. She's a nurse at Central Suffolk Hospital, so you know I'm proud of her. She's my right hand now.

German and I were married for over 60 years. I didn't know how I'd get along without him after he passed. That's his chair over there. Every time I look at it I think of him. German. It was an unusual name, I don't know why his mama named him that.

Sometimes I lay in bed and remember the days of yesteryear. My grandfather, he built the Shiloh Church and you never seen anything so beautiful as the Shiloh Church, so help me God!

— April 12, 1984

Ollie Griffin

Ollie Griffin

Ollie Griffin and his wife, Dorothy, live in South Jamesport near the house where he was born. Now 76 years old and still an avid fisherman, Mr. Griffin says his goal is to be out clamming with his buddies on occasion of his 100th birthday.

I was born here in Jamesport in 1907 in a house where the Cameo Restaurant, or Ken's Place, as some people call it, now stands. Only then it was known as Griffin's Restaurant and my grandfather ran it.

Jamesport was a real going resort town, that's for sure. But that goes back a long time. They had all the boating activities here and five hotels. But they're all gone. None left at all except the one that has the veterans. Such a change. And the shoreline, it was so isolated. Now it's all built up with bungalows, you know.

ONE OF THE FIVE GRAND HOTELS THAT ONCE STOOD IN
SOUTH JAMESPORT.

In those days people didn't get around too much
unless they had a horse, and mostly the horses
belonged to the farmers. So people were pretty well
bottled in. That's why they had lots of time together
— lots of good times.

Over on the corner here they had a place that
showed movin' pictures. Louie Smith operated it in an
open tent without a roof and everytime it rained he'd
have to give you a raincheck. 'Course, there was no
electricity. He had to turn the camera by hand, you
know. And then in the wintertime when things got a
little cold outside, he brought the movies over to our
place.

We showed Buffalo Bill and Tom Mix and I don't
know. It's a long time to remember — but all the old
westerns, mostly. The film would break every once in
awhile and we'd put up the sign, "One Minute Please,"
and he'd patch the film up.

We were all like one big family here, doncha know.
We had the scallop industry and all the men, includin'
myself, worked very hard in it. The scallop houses
were down here on the Jamesport beach and it was the

largest scalloping industry in the United States! We shipped tons of 'em out of here every day. In those days scallops were so plentiful that there never was a question of are there going to be any scallops this year. You just got out your equipment and went scallopin' the first of September.

William Edward had a livery stable down here and he would cart the scallops from the beach, you know, up to the railroad on Washington Avenue. From there they would be shipped out as fast as possible.

When I was a boy I used to go up to the train station with a push cart to get the ice cream for the ice cream parlor we ran at our place. They brought it out from New York City in large tubs packed with ice and salt. It had to be handled fast in order for it not to get soft. Plus we had to keep it without electricity. So we packed it in ice and put salt on it — without salt you can't freeze ice cream. And we sold ice cream like you wouldn't believe.

In the summer we'd hold a big strawberry festival for the village improvement society. We had strawberry shortcake made by the finest bakers, the kind you still find on Sound Avenue today. They have great cooks up there, doncha know. All the people of any age up there are all great cooks. They were born and raised with that background of home cookin' and good food.

Down here we had the same thing. The wife in those days was home cookin' all day and canning while her husband was out scallopin' and making a living that way. And people didn't roam much. They just stuck 'round close to home because there wasn't any way, really, of movin', 'less you got up to the train. And that was the only way you could go anywhere to speak of, doncha know. And I sometimes wonder about all the change . . . When people lived together they were much happier. Maybe the women didn't have all the privileges that they really should have, but that life didn't spell divorce like it does now. What is it? One out of four that get divorced now? And I'm not so sure that number hasn't gone even lower.

My mother was one of 13 children and I was one of five. Her maiden name was Ryan. Old Tom Ryan, my grandfather, he lived to near 100. My mother's name was Aleta. And of course there were 12 brothers and sisters. In my immediate family there was my sister, Vesta, and Howard, Russel, Leon, and me, Oliver, but most people call me Ollie.

My sister Vesta was very popular in the music world. They used to put her in the paper a lot for her wonderful accomplishments — she was a pianist. Played mostly modern and some classic. She liked some of the jazz, too, and she won the piano playing championship of Long Island back in 1915, or'20, I guess. Never had a lesson in her life, but she was a very accomplished musician. And my brother, he had a band for 55 years. He lived right next door, never took lessons either, yet he played just about every instrument you can think of. They grew up with music. Not me, though. I was always stuck with the fix-it end of things. I was youngest, doncha know.

My father was the boss of the H. J. Heinz pickle factory that was located right here where the fertilizer factory is now. It was quite a large operation for those days.

The farmers back then, they didn't have a whole lot of education, you know, and my father, well he did. And he bein' the manager of the plant, he'd go out to the farmers and buy their cauliflower even before it was planted. Contracted for it, you see. And in the fall of the year you would see a double line of horses and wagons loaded to the top with cauliflower goin' from the Jamesport traffic light down to the railroad bridge and into the pickle factory. They'd be loadin' cauliflower there 'til two-o'clock in the morning. They'd put them in these huge tanks, you know, and after they'd got the tank full they'd lock it down with two by fours and fill it with brine. They'd make a brine strong enough to float a potato. That was just the strength that they needed to keep the cauliflower the way they wanted it. After they had it in there for a period of time they'd scoop it out with scoop nets and put it in barrels.

Then the German coopers who we housed over here — we had the men come from Germany to do all the barrel work — then they'd go down to the swamps. You know those barrels had to be made tight so they wouldn't leak. We had cattails in those days — I don't know as you're familiar with 'em. They're gone now, like a lot of other things. And the German coopers would go down to the swamps and bring out huge amounts of those long-stemmed cattail leaves to put between the stavings of the barrels. They'd open them up like an orange and then pull them back with all those leaves in their proper places. Then they'd put the hoops on, bring them back to the factory, and get the barrels ready for the regular putting in of the brine and cauliflower.

My father ran that plant for a good many years. Then he got double pneumonia from workin' underneath the floor. It's awful damp around brine, you know. He was repairin' the pipes. They were all made of wood. All the pipes and barrels were, because metal wouldn't last a long time. And he worked a whole week on 'em and he got pneumonia. Died on Christmas Eve at the age of 49.

After he died they sent out men from the central office in Hicksville and they even had one of my father's understudies run the plant for awhile. But none of them knew how to negotiate with the farmers so the business went downhill and finally it went out. Pop in his heyday made $12 a week. That was the salary for a man of his ability.

My father's father, Captain Tuttle Griffin, came over here from the White Cliffs of Dover. He used to run a big four-masted schooner called the **H. M. Hawkins**. Sailed it all over the ocean with no engine, all sails. He's buried over in the Sound Avenue graveyard. On his stone's written the words, "Friend of the Farmer."

As a bayman, which I think I am, I was born in the water practically. I can say that it was not the sewage that we ever worried about; it's the chlorine that they put in the sewage by the millions of gallons that has caused the collapse of the bay. That's my opinion, speaking as a bayman.

I even wrote a poem about it. They printed it in *The News-Review* about five years ago. Here's a copy of it.

OUR PRECIOUS WATER WAYS

I like to think of the good ole days.
When our streams were crystal clear, and so were our bays.
The seafood was plentiful, the harvesting was hard,
But somehow we did it, and loved it, by God.
In my childhood days, we would walk home from school,

154   **Up-Lot Reveries**

My friends and I,
We'd stop to skip stones in the stream,
as clear as that Monday sky.
I was supposed to gather some water-cress for my mother that
   afternoon,
But I wouldn't have time to get them 'cause I knew I was due home
   soon.
As my friends and I mimicked the frogs jumping lily pad to lily,
The crisp evening air became quite chilly,
As I looked in that clear blue stream, a certain happiness was in
   my heart,
But now, as I look to that same old stream, that joy has broken
   apart.
When they put in the city sewers, I noticed a drastic change.
Into the Peconic River. That's where they put the drain.
Then came the chlorine, chemicals and such.
I suppose at the time it didn't seem like much.
Then in about two years I was really amazed.
This effluent had ruined our rivers and our bay.
It killed our sea grass, the blanket of the sea,
That had always protected our seafood from storms and such, you
   see.
Today we are starting to realize the cost of this carelessness.
And now it changes the water analysis.
As if this error were not enough,
Men then introduced more insurgents,
Pumping in millions of gallons of detergents.
It came out of the cesspolls and underground springs.
Seeping from cesspools,
Complicating all things.
I wrote this poem, the bay to save,
And its precious contents under every wave.

An Oral History of the North Fork   155

You know, history is nothin' more than memories. These are my memories and I love 'em. Always loved it here, too. Traveled an awful lot around the world. My wife and I, we'd go on trips. Still do. Somethin' about the town, though. I've always kinda liked it here.

— August 2, 1984

Hattie Downs
Aldrich

Hattie Downs
Aldrich

Hattie Downs Aldrich has lived all her life in the Riverhead farming community of Northville. Still active at age 92, Mrs. Aldrich now resides with her son, Jack, in the house that she moved into as a bride in 1914.

I was born on Sound Avenue in 1892, in a house that my grandfather, James Downs, built in 1813. 'Course, we had no improvements like you have now. No telephone, no electric lights. It was plain living. But we were just as happy as we are right now. Happier, maybe.

I was the youngest of five sisters. My next-oldest sister was 13 when I born. I don't know how old my mother was when she had me, but she was 15 when she married and she had her first child the following year, so she wasn't very old. Her name was Rachel

Wells Downs and my father was John Tuttle Downs.

My name's Hattie. Always wished it had been Harriet. I don't like Hattie very much. But my sister had a friend named Hattie and well, she was 18 years old when I was born, so my sister was really more like a mother to me and she got to name me. The minister here when I was born was named Reverend Griffith. He was a married man, but had no children and he and his wife badly wanted a baby. So when I was born he came to my parents and asked if they'd let him and his wife have me, seeing as how my folks already had four girls. But my father said well, no, he didn't think he could do that, but that they would give me his name. And that's how I came to be named Hattie Griffith Downs.

I guess the thing I wanted to do most when I was growing up was to get married and have a family. At least for me, I didn't have any ideas about being a teacher or doing some kind of a job. My husband's name was Herman Aldrich. I knew him all the time I was growing up from church, so I didn't have to meet him 'specially. But at some point he took a special interest in me, I guess. We were married at my family home. There were probably 50 people at our wedding. That was in 1914 and people were just beginning to have cars. Now folks seem to think they can't get along without them.

That's one of the changes I've seen over the years. Another one is the way people dress. In those days you never saw anyone going around with nothing much on. And you never saw a woman wearing pants, even though now I can't get along without them. So some of the changes have been for the better.

I always say that you can't change things but

Up-Lot Reveries

sometimes you wish they were more like they used to be. Not everything, of course. But some things. Like the slower way of life we used to have. I think the liquor business is a big cause of a lot of the bad things that are happening. It isn't that people drink, but that they get drunk. Of course, they had liquor back in the old days, but my family didn't drink it. The whole family was WCTU (Woman's Christian Temperance Union) and I still am. Never've touched a drop of alcohol. Not that I know of.

I went to school in the District 10 Schoolhouse. That's the little building that's kind of falling apart on Sound Avenue up near West Lane. I started there when I was five years old. It was all grades in one room. Boys on one side, girls on the other, with a pot-belly stove in the center of the room. We had mostly men teachers but I remember one woman, a Miss Fishburne. Her father was the minister at our church at that time. A nice woman, but, well, I laughed a lot, I guess, when I was younger, and I remember one time she made me stand up in front of the class for laughing too much. It was embarrassing, but I don't recall that I felt too bad about it.

Not too long ago I counted up, and in 1900 there were 50 houses from Roanoke Avenue to the First Parish Church on Sound Avenue and the people in them all were of English descent. All the old names.

We didn't have many tourists passing through in those days, but people used to take in summer boarders from New York. They'd come out on the train and stay for a time. One of them married my great-grandmother's oldest daughter and took her back to New York. She was a seamstress and that's what he had her do. He had her taking in sewing. I don't know if he didn't have any money of his own or he didn't have any job, but anyhow he had her sewing to make money for him. We never thought much of that.

I went to New York when I was a girl to visit my grandmother and my aunt who were living in the city because my aunt was working in a church there. I think we stayed about a week. While we were there my father took me down to the Brooklyn Bridge. It was new then, about 18 years old, I guess. Well, he took me down and we walked across the bridge. It was a great event. Oh, it was wonderful! I've always wanted to go back and walk across it again. Afterwards, we walked downtown and I remember real plain that there were hawkers, I guess you'd call them, trying to sell us things.

We went to the beach a lot when I was young. Swimming? I don't remember swimming. We went bathing in the Sound. Bathing, you just go in the water and kind of jump up and down. And you didn't have to find a bathing suit, you just wore old clothes. The women always used to wear wrappers. I don't know if anyone knows what a wrapper is anymore. It's a long dress more or less like a gown. And it's fitted, not fancy though, just a plain dress. And that's what, if they had an old wrapper, the women would wear to go bathing. I haven't gone to the beach in quite awhile now, but I know what they wear. Nothing! My goodness, the folks back in my childhood days would be shocked to death.

None of the friends my age are still around here. I'm the only old one left. I couldn't tell you how I've managed to live so long, I really don't know. But I never smoked or used alcohol. And I don't take vitamins.

A lot of people in my family lived to be quite old. My father was 92, my mother was 96, and one of my sisters lived to be 100. We grew up eating what we produced ourselves. And I can't remember them using too many chemicals to farm with. They used to use guano for fertilizer. You know what guano is? It's nothing but bird droppings, and they used to bring it from South America to Jamesport on a sloop.

The first thing I can remember them using to kill bugs or anything was Paris Green. They used it to kill potato bugs. It had to be sprinkled on by hand with no machines. My father farmed about 50 acres where the Northville oil tanks now stand. Isn't that something? I often think, what would my father say if he could see those tanks on his farm? They sure made 'em big enough so you could see them. Well, that's progress, I guess.

— *September 27, 1984*

Estelle Evans

Estelle Evans

Known for her creative and sometimes courageous approach to country cooking (fricasseed possum is just one of her many specialties) Estelle Wells Evans has spent most of her life in Northville. She has worked both as a 4-H Cooperative Extension agent and as a teacher at several area schools, including the Riley Avenue school in Calverton where she taught for many years. Now retired, but still active in various historic preservation projects, Mrs. Evans divides her time between her home on Sound Avenue and her late husband's boyhood home in Georgetown, New York.

This house and the land it sits on was known as Terryland back in the days when my grandfather, Herbert Willard Wells, bought it. But the house was no where near as large as it is now, it was just a small rectangular box. Then, bit by bit, my grandfather added on and altered it. The part we're sitting in was built in 1914, so I guess you could call it the new addition.

I was born and grew up here. Isn't that something? When I was teaching school I'd tell my fifth graders that I LIVE in the house where I was born and that would just blow their minds.

I went to school in the Northville school — walked there everyday — and boy, was it fun. We'd go through every deep puddle and all the highest snow banks to see if we'd sink in. And you know, it was a lot better, because by the time we got to school we were ready to sit down and pay attention. Nowadays kids ride the bus, for six miles, some of them, and they're not ready to sit still when they get to school.

My Grandpa Wells was an excellent farmer. He didn't get much education but he read a great deal . . . And talk about a beard! Grandpa always had one. He said a man wasn't a man without a beard. He and Grandma lived in the other part of the house and I remember in the mornings I'd always run over there to watch him make breakfast. I've told a lot of people that I learned to make gravy watching Grandpa Wells. He'd fry a little sausage or bacon, then add a bit of flour and boiling water to the fat and that was it.

But I think my real interest in cooking started, like so many other things, out of necessity. My mother didn't enjoy cooking and I was the oldest daughter, so I ended up doing most of it. Mother would get up in the morning and walk straight out to her garden and stay there all day monkeying around with her flowers. Her name was Sara Helen Wells, but she was called Helen. My father, Leslie Terry Wells, had met her when he was dating her cousin, Irma Reeve. But Irma was not about to get married at the time so my father began

Up-Lot Reveries

dating my mother. She was from a good family and my father put a lot of stock in that. He always used to say that you want to look a little bit at the parents of the person you marry because a lot's passed down.

I guess I'm built like my mother's side of the family, especially my Grandpa Reeve. Perhaps that's how I've managed to stay so slim, despite all the cooking I've done over the years. Grandpa Reeve was a farmer in Mattituck and he lived to be 100. He even drove his car until he was 97. Of course, the traffic wasn't as it is now, but he was alert until the moment he died.

I think I was really fortunate in my life to have done what I aimed at doing. I said I wanted to go to Cornell and become an extension agent and that's what happened. My cousin, Virginia Wines, also went to Cornell, but she's four years younger than me so she was only there one year while I was there.

I remember that in 1938 Virginia and I were supposed to leave for college on September 22 but a hurricane, THE hurricane of '38 came. Oh, it was something weird and very hard to describe to anyone because we were in the eye of it, you see, and the winds first blew real hard from the north, then turned around and came from the south. So for a few minutes we were right in the middle of it, except nobody at the time understood what was going on because there were no hurricane warnings back then. It had rained for ten days before the storm arrived, and when the winds started blowing I was on my way out the door to pick up my sister, Ann, over at the high school. Well, I got there somehow, and we made it home in the nick of time. When my father saw what was happening he told me to go up to the attic to get some old doors to put against the windows on the east side of the house.

And as I started up the attic stairway, I looked out in the front yard and lo and behold, the upper branches of the trees were whirling, sort of spinning around! So I thought, ohhh welll, I guess I've got to get up to the attic anyway, which I did, and just as I got back to one of the east bedrooms with a door, the window in the room exploded! There were itty bitty splinters of glass all over the place, so small you could hardly find them. Then a tree went down in front of the house. Was I terrified? I don't really know that there was much time to be terrified. There was too much to do.

The hurricane lasted all afternoon and we were supposed to leave on the train the next morning, which of course we couldn't do. The scene the next day is hard to describe. We lost 25 trees in our yard. *Twenty-five!* And all along Sound Avenue they were down just like a row of dominoes. There were a lot more trees along Sound Avenue back then. If you go down to the Centerville Chapel and see where the trees sort of canopy over the street, well, it was like that all along the road until the storm took them. It also picked up the cement entrance to our barn out in back and turned it around and there were cemetery stones down all over in Riverhead. Never has been a hurricane like that one. First of all, we weren't warned. And second, you couldn't do anything about all the trees being down because it had rained so much before the storm and the ground was soft. So it was a combination of things. But Aunt Ella was saying the other day that there will be another big one, and likely there will. Then again, things will be entirely different because now we have the communications that we didn't have at that time.

I can't recall ever thinking about leaving the country

life for the city. I think that's because I worked for Cooperative Extension and I listened to all the extension agents at all the meetings saying boy, when they retired what they wanted was a small farm where they could bring their children up in the country. And I thought, yes, then that's a good way to begin, instead of having to go back to it.

My husband, Harold, came from upstate in Madison County, but he was born here on Long Island in Mineola. His father had been an extension agent in Nassau County, and Harold lived there until he was 12 years old. But my own connection with upstate New York began 'way before I met my husband because my father, being a potato farmer, he was always interested in going upstate to see the potato seed farmers. It used to be we could stop our farm work for a week or so in the beginning or middle of July, or whenever the potato tops began to die. We didn't keep irrigating and spraying and so forth. We just went off on a little holiday and let the potatoes die peacefully. Now they keep watering and spraying in hopes of getting a larger crop or a few more per acre, if possible. But we used to leave things be and go visit the seed potato growers up in northern New York State each year in July. Now Harold's father was a seed potato grower, so we went to visit him. Well, I didn't know Harold at the time, so that didn't mean anything. But the fact was that my father knew his father, so that when I met Harold I knew who his family was and that my father respected them and thought that they were good farmers.

I worked as an Extension agent up in Tompkins County before I got married. Both Harold and I wanted to stay in that kind of work and we would have, but World War II came along and he was 1-A in the army. There he was, just out of college and they were ready to ship him overseas. Well, he never did get called, and meanwhile my father needed help down here on the farm because he had no sons, just three daughters. So Harold, who was having a hard time getting hired anythwhere because of his 1-A status for the army, came down here and worked for my father before we were married.

We had four children, two boys and two girls. And Harold liked it very much here because, as my father alway said, Long Island is a place where there are a lot of educated people doing a lot of interesting things. And Harold used to say if Long Island can't solve its problems, probably no other place can. But people still are selfish, I think. For instance, they'll buy a piece of land with no water on it and then demand that there be water on it somehow. They just don't realize that they have an obligation to themselves and society to develop the right spots rather than the wrong ones. You go out to Orient Point where there's salt water intrusion in the ground water. I know for a fact that there are people who have built homes there and had to go across the road to another spot to get water. This insensitivity to nature filters down to all one's being, I think.

The Wells family has been a part of the history of this area for so long because, in my opinion, most of them were concerned about the community and willing to help their neighbors. It probably goes 'way back to when we came from England. The Wells who came over were people who wanted to establish a place that was lasting, a place their families could enjoy. Even some of the ways we talk seems to reach back to those days. For instance, when a man was going out to farm he might say "I'm going up-lot now," or "I'm going down-lot," and you knew he was either headed north or south. I grew up thinking everybody in the world thought that north was up-lot and south was down-lot. I never knew any different.

I remember one time a man came to the door looking to see where Harold was and I said, "He's up-lot," and that didn't mean anything to him so I said, "He's up north, and he says, "Oh, you mean he's gone hunting up in Canada?" Did I ever have a laugh over that! But you know, it never sounded funny to me until that moment.

My cousin Virginia did some research and found out that the word came from the word allotment — that the early settlers had each been granted certain allotments of land at a town meeting in 1661. They had just shortened the word to lot, then added up-lot or down-lot to indicate direction.

You know, back in the old days, from here to Mattituck it was mostly all family along Sound Avenue. Now it's very hard to see the old homes being boarded up or bought by outsiders. It's partly true that we feel a sense of intrusion. But it's not an intrusion if one contributes their time and energy to an area. That kind of person will always be welcome here.